My Christmas Treasury

Norman Vincent Peale

A Giniger Book
published in association with

HarperSanFrancisco
A Division of HarperCollins*Publishers*

MY CHRISTMAS TREASURY. Copyright © 1991 by Norman Vincent Peale. All rights reserved. Published in association with The K. S. Giniger Company, Inc., 250 West 57th Street, New York, NY 10107. Printed in the United States of America. No part of this book may be used or reproduced in any manner whatsoever without written permission except in the case of brief quotations embodied in critical articles and reviews. For information address HarperCollins Publishers,
10 East 53rd Street,
New York, NY 10022.

FIRST EDITION

Library of Congress Cataloging-in-Publication Data

My Christmas treasury / [compiled by] Norman Vincent Peale.—1st ed.
    p.   cm.
    "A Giniger book."
    ISBN 0–06–066686–2 (alk. paper)
    1. Christmas.   I. Peale, Norman Vincent
BV45.M92 1991
242'.23—dc20

91–70041
CIP

91 92 93 94 95 HAD 10 9 8 7 6 5 4 3 2 1

This edition is printed on acid-free paper that meets the American National Standards Institute Z39.48 Standard.

Contents

CONTENTS

Introduction

As I write this, people are worried about the myriad of problems that afflict our world today, and there is no question but that they are very serious problems. Yet everywhere I go, people have smiling faces and happy voices. Streets and shop windows are gaily decorated. The world seems full of familiar music, and there is excitement in the air. Why?

Christmas is coming. Unhappiness seems to be driven from our minds at this season, along with cynicism and gloomy negativism. A strange and wonderful phenomenon is at work; merriment and gaiety fill the air, and a heavenly chorus resounds in our hearts: "Behold, I bring you tidings of great joy" (Luke 2:10).

With the joy of Christmas there also come fond memories of the Bible passages always read to us at this time of year, of the carols and hymns that we have known all our lives and that now fill the air, of the poems and stories bringing us the Christmas spirit.

This little book attempts to collect in one volume some of my own Christmas favorites. Some of them may also be yours; others may be new to you. But they all carry the Bible message of joy, because the

Bible is the happiest book ever written. Jesus told us, "Be of good cheer; I have overcome the world" (John 16:33)—meaning that we, too, can overcome the world. "These things have I spoken unto you . . . that your joy might be full" (John 15:11). And again, "Rejoice," and to make sure that we understand, he repeated, "and again I say, Rejoice" (Philippians 4:4).

I truly believe that if we keep telling the Christmas story, singing the Christmas songs, and living the Christmas spirit, we can bring joy and happiness and peace to this world. I hope that these selections will help you do this.

Merry Christmas to you! May the glory that we celebrate in this Christmas season fill your life forever and ever.

Norman Vincent Peale

My Christmas Treasury

I.
The World's Most Loved Narrative

WHAT A WONDERFUL story it is, the Christmas story. Only God could have thought of it. Here the greatest storytellers of the ages have found their art outmatched. And that story has done more to soften and change humanity than all the stories ever told, all the sermons ever preached, and all the moralisms ever promulgated.

As St. Matthew tells it in the second chapter of his Gospel, it is the story of a star in the east that was observed by some wise scholars. They followed that star for many months, over deserts and mountains and seas, until it came to rest over a little town in a little country. That town was called Bethlehem. There they found an inn, but it was crowded, so they were put in the stable.

The scholars (or wise men or magi, as they were sometimes called) found with them in that stable a young couple with a young baby boy. They who had journeyed so far for so long, following a star, instinctively knew that the baby was immensely important, that he was actually the Son of God. They realized that God, who had tried to win the hearts of men and women in other ways, had finally laid a baby on the doorstep of the world. That baby's crying and cooing were to win the world's heart.

The wise men, representing the intellectuals of the world of that time, fell to their knees before him, recognizing that he, when grown, would be the supreme intellect of all time.

There were some shepherds in a nearby field keeping watch over their flocks by night. Overhead, that chilly night, stretched the star-studded sky. Suddenly the shepherds were startled: a heavenly choir appeared, singing about peace and announcing the birth of the prince of peace. When the shepherds, representing the working people of the world, were told about the birth of the Savior, they said, "Let us now go even unto Bethlehem, and see this thing which is come to pass, which the Lord hath made known unto us" (Luke 2:15, KJV).

And they found the stable and fell to their knees and worshiped God's Son, who had come to earth in the same manner as all men and women—from the heavenly Father, their Creator.

Jesus had come to remind all people that the heavenly Father loved them and to teach them how to live and return ultimately to the Father's House.

In Luke's version of this immortal story (in the second chapter of his Gospel)—a favorite in the King James Version of the

Bible with older people who have loved it since childhood—he features the shepherds; while Matthew, in his first chapter, tells essentially the same story featuring the wise men.

The Birth of Jesus

And it came to pass in those days, that there went out a decree from Caesar Augustus, that all the world should be taxed. (And this taxing was first made when Cyrenius was governor of Syria.) And all went to be taxed, every one into his own city. And Joseph also went up from Galilee, out of the city of Nazareth, into Judea, unto the city of David, which is called Bethlehem, (because he was of the house and lineage of David,) to be taxed with Mary his espoused wife, being great with child.

And so it was, that, while they were there, the days were accomplished that she should be delivered. And she brought forth her firstborn son, and wrapped him in swaddling clothes, and laid him in a manger; because there was no room for them in the inn.

And there were in the same country shepherds abiding in the field, keeping watch over their flock by night. And, lo, the angel of the Lord came upon them, and the glory of the Lord shone round about them; and they were sore afraid. And the angel said unto them, Fear not: for, behold, I bring you good tidings of great joy, which shall be to all people. For unto you is born this day in the city of David a Saviour, which is Christ the Lord. And this shall be a sign unto you; Ye shall find the babe wrapped in swaddling clothes, lying in a manger.

And suddenly there was with the angel a multitude of the heavenly host praising God, and saying, Glory to God in the highest, and on earth peace, good will toward men.

And it came to pass, as the angels were gone away from them into heaven, the shepherds said one to another, Let us now go even unto Bethlehem, and see this thing which is come to pass, which the Lord hath made known unto us. And they came with haste, and found Mary and Joseph, and the babe lying in a manger.

And when they had seen it, they made known abroad the saying which was told them concerning this child. And all they that heard it wondered at those things which were told them by the shepherds.

But Mary kept all these things, and pondered them in her heart.

And the shepherds returned, glorifying and praising God for all the things there they had heard and seen, as it was told unto them.

Luke 2:1–20, (KJV)

Now when Jesus was born in Bethlehem of Judea in the days of Herod the king, behold, there came wise men from the east to Jerusalem, saying, Where is he that is born King of the Jews? for we have seen his star in the east, and are come to worship him.

When Herod the king had heard these things, he was troubled, and all Jerusalem with him. And when he had gathered all the chief priests and scribes of the people together, he demanded of them where Christ should be born.

And they said unto him, In Bethlehem of Judea: for thus it is written by the prophet. And thou Bethlehem, in the land of Juda, art not the least among the princes of Juda; for out of thee shall come a Governor, that shall rule my people Israel.

Then Herod, when he had privily called the wise men, inquired of them diligently what time the star appeared. And he sent them to Bethlehem, and said, Go and search diligently for the young child; and when ye have found him, bring me word again, that I may come and worship him also.

When they had heard the king, they departed; and, lo, the star, which they saw in the east, went before them, till it came and stood over where the young child was. When they saw the star, they rejoiced with exceeding great joy. And when they were come into the house, they saw the young child with Mary his mother, and fell down, and worshipped him: and when they had opened their treasures, they presented unto him gifts; gold, and frankincense, and myrrh.

And being warned of God in a dream that they should not return to Herod, they departed into their own country another way.

Matthew 2:1–12, (KJV)

To repeat this same beloved story in the English language of the present day, here is a modern translation for young readers and their families called the Contemporary English Version. It is translated directly from the Greek original and is not based on any other English translation. The New Testament was made available by the American Bible Society the same year as this book, and the complete Bible is scheduled for publication at a later date.

The Birth of Jesus

This is how Jesus Christ was born. A young woman named Mary was engaged to Joseph from King David's family. But before they were married, she learned that she was going to have a baby by God's Holy Spirit. Joseph was a good man and did not want to embarrass Mary in front of everyone. So he decided to quietly call off the wedding.

While Joseph was thinking about this, an angel from the Lord came to him in a dream. The angel said, "Joseph, the baby that Mary will have is from the Holy Spirit. Go ahead and marry her. Then after her baby is born, name him Jesus, because he will save his people from their sins."

So God's promise came true, just as the prophet had said, "A virgin

will have a baby boy, and he will be called Immanuel," which means "God is with us."

About that time Emperor Augustus gave orders for the names of all the people to be listed in record books. These first records were made when Quirinius was governor of Syria.

Everyone had to go to their own hometown to be listed. So Joseph had to leave Nazareth in Galilee and go to Bethlehem in Judea. Long ago Bethlehem had been King David's hometown, and Joseph went there because he was from David's family.

Mary was engaged to Joseph and traveled with him to Bethlehem. She was soon going to have a baby, and while they were there, she gave birth to her first-born son. She dressed him in baby clothes and laid him in a feed box, because there was no room for them in the inn.

Matthew 1:18–23; Luke 2:1–7, (CEV)

That night in the fields near Bethlehem some shepherds were guarding their sheep. All at once an angel came down to them from the Lord, and the brightness of the Lord's glory flashed around them. The shepherds were frightened. But the angel said, "Don't be afraid! I have good news for you, which will make everyone happy. This very day in King David's hometown a Savior was born for you. He is Christ the

Lord. You will know who he is, because you will find him dressed in baby clothes and lying in a feed box."

Suddenly many other angels came down from heaven and joined in praising God. They said:

> "Praise to God in heaven!
> Peace on earth to everyone
> who pleases God."

After the angels had left and gone back to heaven, the shepherds said to each other, "Let's go to Bethlehem and see what the Lord has told us about." They hurried off and found Mary and Joseph, and they saw the baby lying in the feed box.

When the shepherds saw Jesus, they told his parents what the angel had said about him. Everyone listened and was surprised. But Mary kept thinking about all this and wondered what it meant.

As the shepherds returned to their sheep, they were praising God and saying wonderful things about him. Everything they had seen and heard was just as the angel had said.

Luke 2:8–20, (CEV)

When Jesus was born in the village of Bethlehem in Judea, Herod was king. During this time some wise men from the east came to Jerusalem and said, "Where is the child born to be king of the Jews? We saw his star in the east and have come to worship him."

When King Herod heard about this, he was worried, and so was everyone else in Jerusalem. Herod brought together all the chief priests and the teachers of the Law of Moses and asked them, "Where will the Messiah be born?"

They told him, "He will be born in Bethlehem, just as the prophet wrote,

> 'Bethlehem in the land of Judea,
> you are very important among the towns of Judea.
> From your town will come a leader,
> who will be like a shepherd for my people Israel.' "

Herod secretly called in the wise men and asked them when they had first seen the star. He tod them, "Go to Bethlehem and search carefully for the child. As soon as you find him, let me know. I want to go and worship him, too."

The wise men listened to what the king said and then left. And the star they had seen in the east went on ahead of them until it stopped over the place where the child was. They were thrilled and excited to see the star.

When the men went into the house and saw the child with Mary, his mother, they kneeled down and worshiped him. They took out their gifts of gold, frankincense, and myrrh and gave them to him. Later they were warned in a dream not to return to Herod, and they went back home by another road.

Matthew 2:1–12, (CEV)

II.
Hymns and Carols

*F*OR MOST OF US, the music we hear on the radio, through television, in our churches, and even on the streets at Christmas time is very familiar. We have known these carols and hymns since childhood. The tunes are well known, but we cannot always remember all the words. Yet the words carry a message that goes back a very long time.

"O Come, All Ye Faithful," for example, is the Latin hymn *"Adeste Fideles";* "God Bless the Master of This House" is an old, traditional English carol. And when I was a boy growing up in Cincinnati, which had a large German population, I used to hear the old German Christmas songs, such as *"Stille Nacht,"* which we know as "Silent Night," and *"O Tannenbaum,"* or "O Christmas Tree."

But whatever the original language—Latin, German, or English—the memories these tunes and their words bring back help us keep the joy and freshness and romance and glory of life. They carry the spirit of Jesus, and this brings back deep sentiments and fills us with zest for life.

The old Wanamaker department store, which stood for many years at the corner of Broadway and 9th Street in New York City, was established by John Wanamaker, a Philadelphian who was also a great Christian. In both his Philadelphia and New York stores there was a great wide staircase leading to a balcony, from which a large choir gave a sacred concert every afternoon during the days leading up to Christmas. At the close, the choir led the vast crowd (which invariably assembled) in Christmas carols.

In one Christmas season during the Great Depression of the early 1930s, I met a businessman I knew on the street in New York. He had experienced hard times. "Merry Christmas," I said.

"Now, Norman," he said to me glumly, "what is there to be merry about?"

"Well, Jack," I responded, "God lives and our country will recover. Besides, it's Christmas."

A few days later, I happened to be in Wanamaker's store when the magnificent organ and choir burst into that stirring hymn "O Come, All Ye Faithful." Several thousand people joined in, in one of the most inspiring moments I can recall. Suddenly I saw my friend Jack, with a reverent look on his uplifted countenance. He was singing enthusiastically. I bumped into him at the door later. He had tears in his eyes. All he said was,

"Sure, we'll get through our troubles. Better days are coming."
With a wave of his hand, he was lost in the crowd. Christmas had
given Jack a new lease on life.

Sing these hymns. And if you can't sing, read them.

Come, Thou Long-Expected Jesus

Come, thou long-expected Jesus,
   Born to set thy people free;
From our fears and sins release us,
   Let us find our rest in thee.

Israel's strength and consolation,
   Hope of all the earth thou art;
Dear desire of every nation,
   Joy of every longing heart.

Born thy people to deliver,
    Born a child, and yet a king,
Born to reign in us for ever,
    Now thy gracious kingdom bring.

By thine own eternal Spirit
    Rule in all our hearts alone:
By thine all-sufficient merit
    Raise us to thy glorious throne. Amen.

Charles Wesley, 1744

Adeste Fideles

O come, all ye faithful,
Joyful and triumphant,
O come ye, O come ye to Bethlehem;
Come and behold him,
Born the King of angels;

Refrain
O come, let us adore him,
O come, let us adore him,
O come, let us adore him,
Christ the Lord.

God of God,
Light of Light,
Lo! he abhors not the Virgin's womb:
Very God,
Begotten, not created;
(Refrain)

Sing, choirs of angels,
Sing in exultation,
Sing, all ye citizens of heav'n above;
Glory to God, all glory
In the highest;
(Refrain)

See how the shepherds,
Summoned to his cradle,
Leaving their flocks, draw nigh to gaze;
We too will thither
Bend our joyful footsteps;
(Refrain)

Child, for us sinners,
Poor and in the manger,
We would embrace thee, with love and awe;
Who would not love thee,
Loving us so dearly?
(Refrain)

Yea, Lord, we greet thee,
Born this happy morning;
Jesus, to thee be glory giv'n;
Word of the Father,
Now in flesh appearing;
(Refrain)

Latin carol, 18th century

While Shepherds Watched

While shepherds watch'd their flocks by night,
    All seated on the ground,
The angel of the Lord came down,
    And glory shone around.
"Fear not," said he, for mighty dread
    Had seized their troubled mind;
"Glad tidings of great joy I bring
    To you and all mankind.

"To you, in David's town, this day
    Is born of David's line
The Saviour, who is Christ the Lord;
    And this shall be the sign:
The heav'nly Babe you there shall find
    To human view displayed,
All meanly wrapped in swathing bands,
    And in a manger laid."

Thus spake the seraph, and forthwith
    Appeared a shining throng
Of angels praising God, who thus
    Addressed their joyful song:
"All glory be to God on high
    And on the earth be peace;
Good will henceforth from heav'n to men
    Begin and never cease."

Nahum Tate, 1700

Silent Night

Father Joseph Mohr sat alone working on the sermon he would de-
liver at St. Nicholas Church in Oberndorf in the Austrian Alps on
Christmas Eve, 1818. He was refreshing his mind with the first
Christmas story—"And this shall be a sign unto you: you shall find the
babe . . ."—when a woman knocked at his door and asked him to come
and bless the wife and just-born child of a poor charcoal-maker high up
in the mountains.

The village priest felt a strange exaltation when he arrived at the poor couple's crude hut and found the happy young mother proudly holding her sleeping child. He recalled with a start the words he had been reading when summoned to this primitive bedside: "You shall find the babe."

When midnight mass was over and the last parishioner had called out a cheerful "Gute Nacht!" the priest was still struck with wonder by the charming coincidence of his summons to the bedside in that mountain shack and the Bethlehem mystery celebrated a few hours later. He began to put his thoughts down on paper, and the words became verse. By dawn he had a poem, which he took to Franz Xavier Gruber, a neighboring Arnsdorf music teacher, who on Christmas Day composed the music for "Silent Night." The carol soon became popular in Austria and Germany as "Song from Heaven."

> Silent Night! Holy Night!
> All is calm, all is bright.
> Round yon virgin mother and child!
> Holy Infant so tender and mild,
> Sleep in heavenly peace, sleep in heavenly peace.

Silent Night! Holy Night!
Shepherds quake at the sight!
Glories stream from heaven afar,
Heaven'ly hosts sing Alleluia,
Christ the Saviour is born! Christ the Saviour is born!

Silent Night! Holy Night!
Son of God, love's pure light;
Radiant beams from Thy holy face,
With the dawn of redeeming grace,
Jesus Lord, at Thy birth, Jesus Lord, at Thy birth.

Joseph Mohr, 1818

Hark! the Herald Angels Sing

Hark! the herald angels sing,
 "Glory to the newborn King;
Peace on earth, and mercy mild;
 God and sinners reconciled."

Joyful, all ye nations, rise,
    Join the triumph of the skies;
With the angelic hosts proclaim,
    "Christ is born in Bethlehem."

Refrain
Hark, the herald angels sing,
    "Glory to the newborn King."

Christ, by highest heaven adored;
    Christ, the everlasting Lord:
Late in time behold Him come,
    Offspring of a virgin's womb.
Veiled in flesh the God-head see,
    Hail the incarnate Deity!
Pleased as man with men to appear,
    Jesus our Immanuel here.
(Refrain)

Hail the heavenborn Prince of Peace!
    Hail the Sun of righteousness!

Light and life to all He brings,
  Risen with healing in His wings:
Mild He lays His glory by,
  Born that man no more may die;
Born to raise the sons of earth;
  Born to give them second birth.
(Refrain)

Come, Desire of nations come!
  Fix in us Thy humble home:
Rise, the woman's conquering seed,
  Bruise in us the serpent's head;
Adam's likeness now efface,
  Stamp Thine image in its place:
Second Adam from above,
  Reinstate us in Thy love.
(Refrain)

Charles Wesley, 1739

Noel

It came upon the midnight clear,
    That glorious song of old,
From angels bending near the earth
    To touch their harps of gold:
"Peace on the earth, good will to men,
    From heav'n's all-gracious King."
The world in solemn stillness lay
    To hear the angels sing.

Still through the cloven skies they come
    With peaceful wings unfurled,
And still their heav'nly music floats
    O'er all the weary world;
Above its sad and lowly plains
    They bend on hov'ring wing,
And ever o'er its Babel-sounds
    The blessed angels sing.

Yet with the woes of sin and strife
    The world has suffered long;
Beneath the heav'nly strain have rolled
    Two thousand years of wrong;
And man, at war with man, hears not
    The tidings which they bring;
O hush the noise, ye men of strife,
    And hear the angels sing!

O ye, beneath life's crushing load,
    Whose forms are bending low,
Who toil along the climbing way
    With painful steps and slow,
Look now! for glad and golden hours
    Come swiftly on the wing;
O rest beside the weary road
    And hear the angels sing!

For lo! the days are hast'ning on,
    By prophets seen of old,

When with the ever-circling years
    Shall come the time foretold,
When peace shall over all the earth
    Its ancient splendors fling,
And the whole world give back the song
    Which now the angels sing.

Edmund Hamilton Sears, 1846

God Rest You Merry, Gentlemen

God rest you merry, gentlemen,
    Let nothing you dismay,
Remember Christ our Saviour
    Was born on Christmas Day;
To save us all from Satan's power
    When we were gone astray.

Refrain
O tidings of comfort and joy,
    comfort and joy;
O tidings of comfort and joy!

From God our heav'nly Father
    A blessed angel came;
And unto certain shepherds
    Brought tidings of the same;
How that in Bethlehem was born
    The Son of God by name.
(Refrain)

"Fear not, then," said the angel,
    "Let nothing you affright;
This day is born a Saviour
    Of a pure virgin bright,
To free all those who trust in him
    From Satan's power and might."
(Refrain)

Now to the Lord sing praises,
 All you within this place,
And with true love and brotherhood
 Each other now embrace;
This holy tide of Christmas
 Doth bring redeeming grace.
(Refrain)

London carol, 18th century

O Christmas Tree

O Christmas tree, O Christmas tree,
How lovely are your branches.
In summer sun, in winter snow,
A dress of green you always show.
O Christmas tree, O Christmas tree,
How lovely are your branches.

O Christmas tree, O Christmas tree,
With happiness we greet you.
When decked with candles once a year,
You fill our hearts with yuletide cheer.
O Christmas tree, O Christmas tree,
With happiness we greet you.

Traditional German carol

O Little Town of Bethlehem

O little town of Bethlehem,
      How still we see thee lie!
Above thy deep and dreamless sleep
      The silent stars go by;
Yet in thy dark streets shineth
      The everlasting Light;
The hopes and fears of all the years
      Are met in thee tonight.

For Christ is born of Mary,
    And gathered all above,
While mortals sleep, the angels keep
    Their watch of wond'ring love.
O morning stars, together
    Proclaim the holy birth!
And praises sing to God the King,
    And peace to men on earth.

How silently, how silently,
    The wondrous gift is giv'n!
So God imparts to human hearts
    The blessings of his heav'n.
No ear may hear his coming,
    But in this world of sin,
Where meek souls will receive him still
    The dear Christ enters in.

Where children pure and happy
    Pray to the blessed Child,
Where misery cries out to thee,
    Son of the mother mild;
Where charity stands watching
    And faith holds wide the door,
The dark night wakes, the glory breaks,
    And Christmas comes once more.

O holy Child of Bethlehem!
    Descend to us, we pray;
Cast out our sin and enter in,
    Be born in us today.
We hear the Christmas angels
    The great glad tidings tell;
O come to us, abide with us,
    Our Lord Emmanuel! Amen.

Phillips Brooks, 1867

Christmas Carol

God bless the master of this house,
Likewise the mistress too:
And all the little children
That round the table go.
Love and joy come to you,
And to your wassail too,
And God bless you and send you
A Happy New Year.

Traditional English carol

One of America's most popular poets was inspired by Christmas music to write:

Christmas

I hear along our street
Pass the minstrel throngs;
Hark! they play so sweet,

35

On their hautboys, Christmas songs!
  Let us by the fire
  Ever higher
Sing them till the night expire!

  In December ring
  Every day the chimes;
  Loud the gleemen sing
In the street their merry rhymes.
  Let us by the fire
  Ever higher
Sing them till the night expire!

  Shepherds at the grange,
  Where the Babe was born,
  Sang, with many a change,

Christmas carols until morn.
    Let us by the fire
    Ever higher
Sing them till the night expire!

           Henry Wadsworth Longfellow, 1847

III.
Poems and Songs

*W*HEN I WAS growing up, children were made to take elocution lessons, in the course of which they had to memorize poems. (Not all of the verses, to be sure, could be dignified by the name poetry.) These poems would then be recited, with appropriate gestures, to admiring audiences of family and relatives. This custom seems to have vanished, but for those of us who survived the experience, the lines of poetry we learned then remain with us still.

Because family gatherings at Christmas were favorite occasions for such recitations, many of the verses dealt with Christmas, and two of those favorites are here: Eugene Field's "Jest 'Fore Christmas" and Clement C. Moore's "A Visit from St. Nicholas," popularly known as "The Night Before Christmas."

"Jingle Bells," of course, continues to be the all-time favorite Christmas song, and no herd of red-nosed reindeer or longings for a white Christmas can displace it.

Memories of songs and poems such as these can keep Christmases past fresh within you and help you feel young again in spirit, even though you may be adding up your years.

*Eugene Field was a Chicago newspaper columnist. Three of his poems,
"Little Boy Blue," "Wynken, Blynken, and Nod," and this one were
recited in almost every household when I was a boy.*

Jest 'Fore Christmas

Father calls me William, sister calls me Will,
Mother calls me Willie, but the fellers call me Bill!
Mighty glad I ain't a girl—ruther be a boy,
Without them sashes, curls, an' things that's worn by Fauntleroy!
Love to chawnk green apples an' go swimmin' in the lake—
Hate to take the castor-ile they give for belly-ache!
'Most all the time, the whole year round, there ain't no flies on me,
But jest 'fore Christmas I'm as good as I kin be!

Got a yeller dog named Sport, sic him on a cat;
First thing she knows she doesn't know where she is at!
Got a clipper sled, an' when us kids goes out to slide,
'Long comes the grocery cart, an' we all hook a ride!
But sometimes when the grocery man is worrited an' cross,

He reaches at us with his whip, an' larrups up his hoss,
An' then I laff and holler, "Oh, ye never teched me!"
But jest 'fore Christmas I'm as good as I kin be!

Gran'ma says she hopes that when I git to be a man,
I'll be a missionarer like her oldest brother, Dan,
As was et up by the cannibuls that lives in Ceylon's Isle,
Where every prospeck pleases, an' only man is vile!

But Gran'ma she has never been to see a Wild West show,
Not read the Life of Daniel Boone, or else I guess she'd know
That Buff'lo Bill an' cowboys is good enough for me!
Excep' just 'fore Christmas when I'm good as I kin be!

And then old Sport he hangs around, so solemn-like an' still
His eyes they seem a'sayin': "What's the matter, little Bill?"
The old cat sneaks down off her perch an' wonders what's become

Of them two enemies of hern that used to make things hum!
But I am so perlite an' tend to earnestly to biz,
That mother says to father: "How improved our Willie is!"
But father, havin' been a boy hisself, suspicions me
When, jest 'fore Christmas I'm as good as I kin be!

For Christmas, with its lots an' lots of candles, cakes, an' toys,
Was made, they says, for proper kids an' not for naughty boys;
So wash yer face an' bresh yer hair, an' mind yer p's and q's,
An' don't bust out yer pantaloons, an' don't wear out yer shoes;
Say "Yessum" to the ladies, an' "Yessir" to the men,
An' when they's company, don't pass yer plate for pie again;
But, thinkin' of the things yer'd like to see upon that tree,
Jest 'fore Christmas be as good as yer kin be!

Eugene Field, 1892

43

A Christmas Song

Everywhere, everywhere, Christmas to-night!
Christmas in lands of fir tree and pine;
Christmas in lands of palm tree and vine;
Christmas where snow peaks stand solemn and white;
Christmas where cornfields lie sunny and bright:
    Everywhere, everywhere, Christmas to-night!

Christmas where children are hopeful and gay;
Christmas where old men are patient and gray;
Christmas where peace, like a dove in its flight,
Broods o'er brave men in the thick of the fight:
    Everywhere, everywhere, Christmas to-night!

Then let every heart keep its Christmas within,
Christ's pity for sorrow, Christ's hatred for sin,
Christ's care for the weakest, Christ's courage for right,
Christ's dread of the darkness, Christ's love of the light,
    Everywhere, everywhere, Christmas to-night!

Phillips Brooks, 1879

44

Jingle Bells

Dashing thro' the snow in a one-horse open sleigh,
O'er the fields we go, laughing all the way;
Bells on bob-tail ring, making spirits bright;
What fun it is to ride and sing a sleighing song tonight!

Refrain
Jingle bells! Jingle bells! Jingle all the way!
Oh! what fun it is to ride in a one-horse open sleigh!

A day or two ago I thought I'd take a ride,
And soon Miss Fanny Bright was seated by my side;
The horse was lean and lank, misfortune seemed his lot,
He got into a drifted bank, and we, we got upsot.
(Refrain)

Now the ground is white, go it while you're young,
Take the girls tonight, and sing this sleighing song;
Just get a bob-tailed nag, two-forty for his speed,
Then hitch him to an open sleigh, and crack! you'll take the lead.
(Refrain)

John Pierpont, 1827

A Visit from St. Nicholas

'Twas the night before Christmas, when all through the house
Not a creature was stirring, not even a mouse;
The stockings were hung by the chimney with care,
In hopes that St. Nicholas soon would be there.
The children were nestled all snug in their beds,
While visions of sugar-plums danced in their heads;
And mamma in her kerchief, and I in my cap,
Had just settled our brains for a long winter's nap;
When out on the lawn there arose such a clatter,

I sprang from my bed to see what was the matter.
Away to the window I flew like a flash,
Tore open the shutters and threw up the sash.
The moon on the breast of the new-fallen snow
Gave the luster of midday to objects below,
When, what to my wondering eyes should appear,
But a miniature sleigh and eight tiny reindeer,

With a little old driver, so lively and quick,
I knew in a moment it must be St. Nick.
More rapid than eagles his coursers they came,
And he whistled, and shouted, and called them by name:
"Now, Dasher! now, Dancer! now, Prancer and Vixen!
On Comet! on, Cupid! on, Donder and Blitzen!
To the top of the porch, to the top of the wall!
Now, dash away! dash away! dash away all!"
As dry leaves that before the wild hurricane fly,
When they meet with an obstacle, mount to the sky,
So up to the house-top the coursers they flew,
With the sleigh full of toys, and St. Nicholas, too.
And then, in a twinkling, I heard on the roof
The prancing and pawing of each little hoof.
As I drew in my head, and was turning around,
Down the chimney St. Nicholas came with a bound.
He was dressed all in fur, from his head to his foot,
And his clothes were all tarnished with ashes and soot;
A bundle of toys he had flung on his back,
And he looked like a peddler just opening his pack.
His eyes—how they twinkled! his dimples, how merry!

His cheeks were like roses, his nose like a cherry.
His droll little mouth was drawn up like a bow,
And the beard of his chin was as white as the snow.
The stump of a pipe he held tight in his teeth,
And the smoke it encircled his head like a wreath.
He had a broad face and a little round belly
That shook, when he laughed, like a bowlful of jelly.
He was chubby and plump, a right jolly old elf,
And I laughed when I saw him, in spite of myself.
A wink of his eye and a twist of his head
Soon gave me to know I had nothing to dread.
He spoke not a word, but went straight to his work,
And filled all the stockings; then turned with a jerk,
And laying his finger aside of his nose,
And giving a nod, up the chimney he rose.
He sprang to his sleigh, to his team gave a whistle,
And away they all flew like the down of a thistle.
But I heard him exclaim, ere he drove out of sight,
"Happy Christmas to all, and to all a good-night!"

Clement C. Moore, 1823

49

Christmas Bells

I heard the bells on Christmas Day
Their old, familiar carols play,
  And wild and sweet
  The words repeat
Of peace on earth, good-will to men!

And thought how, as the day had come,
The belfries of all Christendom
  had rolled along
  The unbroken song
Of peace on earth, good-will to men!

Till, ringing, singing on its way,
The world revolved from night to day,
  A voice, a chime,
  A chant sublime
Of peace on earth, good-will to men!

Then from each black, accursed mouth
The cannon thundered in the South,
    And with the sound
    The carols drowned
Of peace on earth, good-will to men!

It was as if an earthquake rent
The hearth-stones of a continent
    And made forlorn
    The households born
Of peace on earth, good-will to men!

And in despair I bowed my head;
"There is no peace on earth," I said;
    "For hate is strong,
    And mocks the song
Of peace on earth, good-will to men!"

Then pealed the bells more loud and deep:
"God is not dead; nor doth He sleep!
    The Wrong shall fail,

The Right prevail,
With peace on earth, good-will to men!"

Henry Wadsworth Longfellow, 1861

Somehow

Somehow not only for Christmas
But all the long year through,
The joy that you give to others
Is the joy that comes back to you.
And the more you spend in blessing
The poor and lonely and sad,
The more of your heart's possessing
Returns to make you glad.

John Greenleaf Whittier, 1866

Christmas Day and Every Day

> Star high,
> Baby low:
> 'Twixt the two
> Wise men go;
> Find the baby,
> Grasp the star—
> Heirs of all things
> Near and far!

George MacDonald, 1855

The Three Ships

As I went up the mountain-side
The sea below me glitter'd wide,
And, Eastward, far away, I spied
    On Christmas Day, on Christmas Day,
The three great ships that take the tide
    On Christmas Day in the morning.

Ye have heard the song, how these must ply
From the harbours of home to the ports o' the sky!
Do ye dream none knoweth the whither and why
    On Christmas Day, on Christmas Day,
The three great ships go sailing by
    On Christmas Day in the morning?

Yet, as I live, I never knew
That ever a song could ring so true,
Till I saw them break thro' a haze of blue
    On Christmas Day, on Christmas Day;
And the marvellous ancient flags they flew
    On Christmas Day in the morning!

From the heights above the belfried town
I saw that the sails were patched and brown,
But the flags were a-flame with a great renown
    On Christmas Day, on Christmas Day,
And on every mast was a golden crown
    On Christmas Day in the morning.

Most marvellous ancient ships were these!
Were their prows a-plunge to the Chersonese,
For the pomp of Rome, of the glory of Greece,
    On Christmas Day, on Christmas Day?
Were they out on a quest for the Golden Fleece
    On Christmas Day in the morning?

The sun and the wind they told me there
How goodly a load the three ships bear,
For the first is gold and the second is myrrh
    On Christmas Day, on Christmas Day;
And the third is frankincense most rare,
    On Christmas Day in the morning.

They have mixed their shrouds with the golden sky,
They have faded away where the last dreams die . . .
Ah yet, will ye watch, when the mist lifts high
    On Christmas Day, on Christmas Day?

Will ye see three ships come sailing by
   On Christmas Day in the morning?

Alfred Noyes, 1907

I have personal memories of poet Edwin Markham in his latter years, a white-haired genial giant. Some thought he looked like Santa Claus. During a never-to-be-forgotten evening with him, I asked which of his poems he valued the most. He answered, "How can you choose between your own children?" He added that these four lines called "Outwitted" might have more lasting qualities than some of his others, because love itself lasts.

> He drew a circle that shut me out—
> Heretic, rebel, a thing to flout.
> But Love and I had the wit to win:
> We drew a circle that took him in!

He was a lovable man. I often used the following poem by him in my Christmas sermons at Marble Collegiate Church.

How the Great Guest Came

Before the Cathedral in grandeur rose
At Ingelburg where the Danube goes
Before its forest of silver spires
Went airily up the clouds and fires;
Before the oak had ready a beam,
While yet the arch was stone and dream—
There where the altar was later laid,
Conrad, the cobbler, plied his trade.

. . . .

It happened one day at the year's white end,
Two neighbors called on their old-time friend;
And they found the shop, so meager and mean,
Made gay with a hundred boughs of green.
Conrad was stitching with face ashine,
But suddenly stopped as he twitched a twine:
"Old friends, good news! At dawn today,
As the cocks were scaring the night away,

57

The Lord appeared in a dream to me,
And said, 'I am coming your Guest to be!'
So I've been busy with feet astir,
Strewing the floor with branches of fir.
The wall is washed and the shelf is shined,
And over the rafter the holly twined.
He comes today, and the table is spread
With milk and honey and wheaten bread."

His friends went home; and his face grew still
As he watched for the shadow across the sill.
He lived all the moments o'er and o'er
When the Lord should enter the lowly door—
The knock, the call, the latch pulled up,
The lighted face, the offered cup.
He would wash the feet where the spikes had been,
He would kiss the hands where the nails went in,
And then at last would sit with Him
And break the bread as the day grew dim.

While the cobbler mused there passed his pane
A beggar drenched by the driving rain.
He called him in from the stony street
And gave him shoes for his bruised feet.
The beggar went and there came a crone,
Her face with wrinkles of sorrow sown.
A bundle of fagots bowed her back,
And she was spent with the wrench and rack.
He gave her his loaf and steadied her load
As she took her way on the weary road.
Then to his door came a little child,
Lost and afraid in the world so wild,
In the big, dark world. Catching it up,
He gave it the milk in the waiting cup,
And let it come to its mother's arms,
Out of the reach of the world's alarms.

The day went down in the crimson west
And with it the hope of the blessed Guest,
And Conrad sighed as the world turned gray:
"Why is it, Lord, that your feet delay?

Did You forget that this was the day?"
Then soft in the silence a Voice he heard:
"Lift up your heart, for I kept my word.
Three times I came to your friendly door;
Three times my shadow was on your floor.
I was the beggar with the bruised feet;
I was the woman you gave to eat;
I was the child on the homeless street!"

Edwin Markham, 1899

A Christmas List

"Ask," He said, "and you shall receive."
When you're nine years old, your heart can believe.
"Give me a doll that drinks and sleeps."
I asked, but oh, I didn't receive.

"Ask," He said, "and you shall receive."
I was young and in love, it was Christmas Eve.
"Give me the heart of that special boy."
I asked, but oh, I didn't receive.

"Ask," He said, "and you shall receive."
Money was scarce but I tried to believe.
"Give us enough for the gifts on our list."
I asked, but oh, I didn't receive.

"Ask," He said, "and you shall receive."
Sorting my values, I began to perceive.
"Give me Your Son. Let Him shine through me."
I asked, and lo, I began to receive . . .

More than I'd ever dared to believe—
Treasures unmeasured, blessings undreamed,
All I'd asked or hoped to achieve.
"Ask," He said, "and you shall receive."

Marilyn Morgan Helleberg, 1982

The Glory of Christmas

Give thanks to the baby asleep in the hay,
For it's Jesus who gave us our first Christmas Day.
A king in disguise, God sent Him to men,
Revealed to our hearts, He comes again.

Lord of the galaxies as well as our earth,
A hymn of the Universe celebrates His birth.
He gives us His Spirit, His kingdom's within,
His peace can be ours by believing in Him.

His truth is a flame that ignites young souls,
He is comfort to men for whom the bell tolls,
He restores an image both marred and grown dim,
He's a constant wonder to those who love Him.

As we wrap up our presents to give them away,
We do this because of that first Christmas Day,

When the Lord of all glory and beauty and wealth
Came to earth as a Baby to give us Himself.

Laverne Riley O'Brien, 1982

The Love That Lives

Every child on earth is holy,
Every crib is a manger lowly,
Every home is a stable dim,
Every kind word is a hymn,
Every star is God's own gem,
And every town is Bethlehem,
For Christ is born and born again,
When His love lives in hearts of men.

W. D. Dorrity, 1909

The Priceless Gift of Christmas

The Priceless Gift of Christmas
Is meant just for the heart
And we receive it only
When we become a part
Of the kingdom and the glory
Which is ours to freely take.
For God sent the Holy Christ Child
At Christmas for our sake,
So man might come to know Him
And feel His Presence near
And see the many miracles.
And this Priceless Gift of Christmas
Is within the reach of all,
The rich, the poor, the young and old
The greatest and the small.

So take His Priceless Gift of Love,
Reach out and you receive,
And the only payment that God asks
Is just that you believe.

Helen Steiner Rice, 1970

IV.
Christmas
Stories

COUNTLESS STORIES with Christmas as their theme have been published, and selecting from among them is difficult. Although Harriet Beecher Stowe is well remembered for *Uncle Tom's Cabin,* her "Christmas; Or, The Good Fairy," with its sentimental note, may be new to you. On the other hand, it is Henry Van Dyke's two Christmas stories that have kept his reputation alive. O. Henry's "Gift of the Magi" continues to be performed as a play in many cities each Christmas, as well as on television. And Charles Dickens's "A Christmas Carol" remains an all-time favorite. Franklin Delano Roosevelt, whether spending Christmas at Hyde Park or in the White House, used to gather his family around him each Christmas Eve and read the Dickens story to them. Unfortunately, space allows me to include here only its last three paragraphs.

Each of these selections has, as do all Christmas stories, a moral best expressed in the last words of Van Dyke's "The First Christmas Tree": "Good-will, henceforth, from heaven to men begin and never cease."

When you think of Charles Dickens's Scrooge, do you recall his being mean and miserable and miserly? Why not remember him as Dickens left him in the closing paragraphs of "A Christmas Carol"?

From "A Christmas Carol"

"A merry Christmas, Bob!" said Scrooge, with an earnestness that could not be mistaken, as he clapped him on the back. "A merrier Christmas, Bob, my good fellow, than I have given you for many a year! I'll raise your salary, and endeavor to assist your struggling family, and we will discuss your affairs this very afternoon, over a Christmas bowl of smoking bishop, Bob! Make up the fires, and buy another coal-scuttle before you dot another *i,* Bob Cratchit!"

Scrooge was better than his word. He did it all, and infinitely more; and to Tiny Tim, who did NOT die, he was a second father. He became as good a friend, as good a master, and as good a man, as the good old city knew, or any other good old city, town, or borough, in the good old world. Some people laughed to see the alteration in him, but he let them laugh, and little heeded them; for he was wise enough to know that nothing ever happened on this globe, for good, at which some people did not have their fill of laughter in the outset; and knowing that such as these would be blind anyway, he thought it quite as well that they should wrinkle up their eyes in grins, as have the malady in less attractive forms. His own heart laughed: and that was quite enough for him.

He had no further intercourse with Spirits, but lived upon the Total Abstinence Principle, ever afterwards; and it was always said of him, that he knew how to keep Christmas well, if any man alive possessed the knowledge. May that be truly said of us, and all of us! And so, as Tiny Tim observed, God Bless Us, Every One!

Charles Dickens, 1843

Christmas; Or, The Good Fairy

"Oh, dear! Christmas is coming in a fortnight, and I have got to think up presents for everybody!" said young Ellen Stuart, as she leaned languidly back in her chair. "Dear me, it's so tedious! Everybody has got everything that can be thought of."

"Oh, no," said her confidential adviser, Miss Lester, in a soothing tone. "You have means of buying everything you can fancy; and when every shop and store is glittering with all manner of splendors, you cannot surely be at a loss."

"Well, now, just listen. To begin with, there's mamma. What can I get for her? I have thought of ever so many things. She has three card cases, four gold thimbles, two or three gold chains, two writing desks of different patterns; and then as to rings, brooches, boxes, and all other things, I should think she might be sick of the sight of them. I am sure I am," said she, languidly gazing on her white and jeweled fingers.

This view of the case seemed rather puzzling to the adviser, and there was silence for a few minutes, when Ellen, yawning, resumed: "And then there's cousins Jane and Mary; I suppose they will be coming down on me with a whole load of presents; and Mrs. B. will send me something—she did last year; and then there's cousins William and Tom—I must get them something; and I would like to do it well enough, if I only knew what to get."

"Well," said Eleanor's aunt, who had been sitting quietly rattling her knitting needles during this speech, "it's a pity that you had not such a subject to practice on as I was when I was a girl. Presents did not fly about in those days as they do now. I remember, when I was ten years old, my father gave me a most marvelously ugly sugar dog for a Christmas gift, and I was perfectly delighted with it, the very idea of a present was so new to us."

"Dear aunt, how delighted I should be if I had any such fresh, unsophisticated body to get presents for! But to get and get for people that have more than they know what to do with now; to add pictures, books, and gilding when the center tables are loaded with them now, and rings and jewels when they are a perfect drug! I wish myself that I were not sick, and sated, and tired with having everything in the world given me."

"Well, Eleanor," said her aunt, "if you really do want unsophisticated subjects to practice on, I can put you in the way of it. I can show you more than one family to whom you might seem to be a very good fairy, and where such gifts as you could give with all ease would seem like a magic dream."

"Why, that would really be worth while, aunt."

"Look over in that back alley," said her aunt. "You see those buildings?"

"That miserable row of shanties? Yes."

"Well, I have several acquaintances there who have never been tired of Christmas gifts or gifts of any other kind. I assure you, you could make quite a sensation over there."

"Well, who is there? Let us know."

"Do you remember Owen, that used to make your shoes?"

"Yes, I remember something about him."

71

"Well, he has fallen into a consumption, and cannot work anymore; and he, and his wife, and three little children live in one of the rooms."

"How do they get along?"

"His wife takes in sewing sometimes, and sometimes goes out washing. Poor Owen! I was over there yesterday; he looks thin and wasted, and his wife was saying that he was parched with constant fever, and had very little appetite. She had, with great self-denial, and by restricting herself almost of necessary food, got him two or three oranges; and the poor fellow seemed so eager after them."

"Poor fellow!" said Eleanor, involuntarily.

"Now," said her aunt, "suppose Owen's wife should get up on Christmas morning and find at the door a couple dozen of oranges, and some of those nice white grapes, such as you had at your party last week; don't you think it would make a sensation?"

"Why, yes, I think very likely it might; but who else, aunt? You spoke of a great many."

"Well, on the lower floor there is a neat little room, that is always kept perfectly trim and tidy; it belongs to a young couple who have nothing beyond the husband's day wages to live on. They are, nevertheless, as cheerful and chipper as a couple of wrens; and she is up and down half a dozen times a day, to help poor Mrs. Owen. She has a baby of her own about five months old, and of course does all the cooking, washing, and ironing for herself and husband; and yet, when Mrs. Owen goes out to wash, she takes her baby, and keeps it whole days for her."

"I'm sure she deserves that the good fairies should smile on her," said Eleanor; "one baby exhausts my stock of virtues very rapidly."

"But you ought to see her baby," said Aunt E.; "so plump, so rosy, and good-natured, and always clean as a lily. This baby is a sort of household shrine; nothing is too sacred or too good for it; and I believe the little thrifty woman feels only one temptation to be extravagant, and that is to get some ornaments to adorn this little divinity."

"Why, did she ever tell you so?"

"No; but one day, when I was coming down stairs, the door of their room was partly open, and I saw a peddler there with open box. John, the husband, was standing with a little purple cap on his hand, which he was regarding with mystified, admiring air, as if he didn't quite comprehend it, and trim little Mary gazing at it with longing eyes.

"'I think we might get it,' said John.

"'Oh, no,' said she, regretfully; 'yet I wish we could, it's so pretty!'"

"Say no more, aunt. I see the good fairy must pop a cap into the window on Christmas morning. Indeed, it shall be done. How they

73

will wonder where it came from, and talk about it for months to come!"

"Well, then," continued her aunt, "in the next street to ours there is a miserable building, that looks as if it were just going to topple over; and away up in the third story, in a little room just under the eaves, live two poor, lonely old women. They are both nearly on to ninety. I was in there day before yesterday. One of them is constantly confined to her bed with rheumatism; the other, weak and feeble, with failing sight and trembling hands, totters about, her only helper; and they are entirely dependent on charity."

"Can't they do anything? Can't they knit?" said Eleanor.

"You are young and strong, Eleanor, and have quick eyes and nimble fingers; how long would it take you to knit a pair of stockings?"

"I?" said Eleanor. "What an idea! I never tried, but I think I could get a pair done in a week, perhaps."

"And if somebody gave you twenty-five cents for them, and out of this you had to get food, and pay room rent, and buy coal for your fire, and oil for your lamp—"

"Stop, aunt, for pity's sake!"

"Well, I will stop; but they can't: they must pay so much every month for that miserable shell they live in, or be turned into the street. The meal and flour that some kind person sends goes off for them just as it does for others, and they must get more or starve; and coal is now scarce and high priced."

"O aunt, I'm quite convinced, I'm sure; don't run me down and annihilate me with all these terrible realities. What shall I do to play good fairy to these old women?"

"If you will give me full power, Eleanor, I will put up a basket to be sent to them that will give them something to remember all winter."

"Oh, certainly I will. Let me see if I can't think of something myself."

"Well, Eleanor, suppose, then, some fifty or sixty years hence, if you were old, and if your father, and mother, and aunts, and uncles, now so thick around you, lay cold and silent in so many graves—you have somehow got away off to a strange city, where you were never known—you live in a miserable garret, where snow blows at night through the cracks, and the fire is very apt to go out in the old cracked stove—you sit crouching over the dying embers the evening before Christmas—nobody to speak to you, nobody to care for you, except another poor soul who lies moaning in the bed. Now, what would you like to have sent you?"

"Oh aunt, what a dismal picture!"

"And yet, Ella, all poor, forsaken old women are made of young girls, who expected it in their youth as little as you do, perhaps."

"Say no more, aunt. I'll buy—let me see—a comfortable warm shawl for each of these poor women; and I'll send them—let me see—oh, some tea—nothing goes down with old women like tea; and I'll make John wheel some coal over to them; and, aunt, it would not be a very bad thought to send them a new stove. I remember, the other day, when mamma was pricing stoves, I saw some such nice ones for two or three dollars."

"For a new hand, Ella, you work up the idea very well," said her aunt.

"But how much ought I to give, for any one case, to these women, say?"

"How much did you give last year for any single Christmas present?"

"Why, six or seven dollars for some; those elegant souvenirs were seven dollars; that ring I gave Mrs. B. was twenty."

"And do you suppose Mrs. B. was any happier for it?"

"No, really, I don't think she cared much about it; but I had to give her something, because she had sent me something the year before, and I did not want to send a paltry present to one in her circumstances."

"Then, Ella, give the same to any poor, distressed, suffering creature who really needs it, and see in how many forms of good such a sum will appear. That one hard, cold, glittering ring, that now cheers nobody, and means nothing, that you give because you must, and she takes because she must, might, if broken up into smaller sums, send real warm and heartfelt gladness through many a cold and cheerless dwelling, through many an aching heart."

"You are getting to be an orator, aunt; but don't you approve of Christmas presents, among friends and equals?"

"Yes, indeed," said her aunt, fondly stroking her head. "I have had some Christmas presents that did me a world of good—a little book mark, for instance, that a certain niece of mine worked for me, with wonderful secrecy, three years ago, when she was not a young lady with a purse full of money—that book mark was a true Christmas present; and my young couple across the way are plotting a profound surprise to each other on Christmas morning. John has contrived, by an hour of extra work every night, to lay by enough to get Mary a new calico dress; and she, poor soul, has bargained away the only thing in the jewelry line she ever possessed, to be laid out on a new hat for him.

"I know, too, a washerwoman who has a poor lame boy—a patient, gentle little fellow—who has lain quietly for weeks and months in his little crib, and his mother is going to give him a splendid Christmas present."

"What is it, pray?"

77

"A whole orange! Don't laugh. She will pay ten whole cents for it; for it shall be none of your common oranges, but a picked one of the very best going! She has put by the money, a cent at a time, for a whole month; and nobody knows which will be happiest in it, Willie or his mother. These are such Christmas presents as I like to think of—gifts coming from love, and tending to produce love; these are the appropriate gifts of the day."

"But don't you think that it's right for those who *have* money to give expensive presents, supposing always, as you say, they are given from real affection?"

"Sometimes, undoubtedly. The Saviour did not condemn her who broke an alabaster box of ointment—very precious—simply as a proof of love, even although the suggestion was made, 'This might have been sold for three hundred pence, and given to the poor.' I have thought he would regard with sympathy the fond efforts which human love sometimes makes to express itself by gifts, the rarest and most costly. How I rejoiced with all my heart, when Charles Elton gave his poor mother that splendid Chinese shawl and gold watch! because I knew they came from the very fullness of his heart to a mother that he could not do too much for—a mother that has done and suffered everything for him. In some such cases, when resources are ample, a costly gift seems to have a graceful appropriateness; but I cannot approve of it if it exhausts all the means of doing for the poor; it is better, then, to give a simple offering, and to do something for those who really need it."

Eleanor looked thoughtful; her aunt laid down her knitting, and said, in a tone of gentle seriousness, "Whose birth does Christmas commemorate, Ella?"

"Our Saviour's, certainly, aunt."

"Yes," said her aunt. "And when and how was he born? In a stable! laid in a manger; thus born, that in all ages he might be known as the brother and friend of the poor. And surely, it seems but appropriate to commemorate his birthday by an especial remembrance of the lowly, the poor, the outcast, and distressed; and if Christ should come back to our city on a Christmas day, where should we think it most appropriate to his character to find him? Would he be carrying splendid gifts to splendid dwellings, or would he be gliding about in the cheerless haunts of the desolate, the poor, the forsaken, and the sorrowful?"

And here the conversation ended.

"What sort of Christmas presents is Ella buying?" said Cousin Tom, as the servant handed in a portentous-looking package, which had been just run in at the door.

"Let's open it," said saucy Will. "Upon my word, two great gray blanket shawls! These must be for you and me, Tom! And what's this? A great bolt of cotton flannel and gray yarn stockings!"

The door bell rang again, and the servant brought in another bulky parcel, and deposited it on the marble-topped centre table.

"What's here?" said Will, cutting the cord. "Whew! a perfect nest of packages! Oolong tea! oranges! grapes! white sugar! Bless me, Ella must be going to housekeeping!"

"Or going crazy!" said Tom; "and on my word," said he, looking out of the window, "there's a drayman ringing at our door, with a stove, with a teakettle set in the top of it!"

"Ella's cook stove, of course," said Will; and just at this moment the young lady entered, with her purse hanging gracefully over her hand.

"Now, boys, you are too bad!" she exclaimed, as each of the mischievous youngsters was gravely marching up and down, attired in a gray shawl.

"Didn't you get them for us? We thought you did," said both.

"Ella, I want some of that cotton flannel, to make me a pair of pantaloons," said Tom.

"I say, Ella," said Will, "when are you going to housekeeping? Your cooking stove is standing down in the street; 'pon my word, John is loading some coal on the dray with it."

"Ella, isn't that going to be sent to my office?" said Tom; "do you know I do so languish for a new stove with a teakettle in the top, to heat a fellow's shaving-water!"

Just then, another ring at the door, and the grinning servant handed in a small brown paper parcel for Miss Ella. Tom made a dive at it, and tearing off the brown paper, discovered a jaunty little purple velvet cap, with silver tassels.

"My smoking cap, as I live!" said he; "only I shall have to wear it on my thumb, instead of my head—too small entirely," said he, shaking his head gravely.

"Come, you saucy boys," said Aunt E., entering briskly. "What are you teasing Ella for?"

"Why, do you see this lot of things, aunt! What in the world is Ella going to do with them?"

"Oh, I know!"

"You know! Then I can guess, aunt, it is some of your charitable works. You are going to make a juvenile Lady Bountiful of El, eh?"

Ella, who had colored to the roots of her hair at the exposé of her very unfashionable Christmas preparations, now took heart, and bestowed a very gentle and salutary little cuff on the saucy head that still wore the purple cap, and then hastened to gather up her various purchases.

"Laugh away," said she, gayly; "and a good many others will laugh, too, over these things. I got them to make people laugh—people that are not in the habit of laughing!"

"Well, well, I see into it," said Will; "and I tell you I think right well of the idea, too. There are worlds of money wasted, at this time of the year, in getting things that nobody wants, and nobody cares for after they are got; and I am glad, for my part, that you are going to get up a variety in this line; in fact, I should like to give you one of these stray leaves to help on," said he, dropping a ten dollar note into her paper. "I like to encourage girls to think of something besides breastpins and sugar candy."

But our story spins on too long. If anybody wants to see the results of Ella's first attempts at *good fairyism,* they can call at the doors of two or three old buildings on Christmas morning, and they shall hear all about it.

Harriet Beecher Stowe, 1869

The Story of the Other Wise Man

THE SIGN IN THE SKY

In the days when Augustus Caesar was master of many kings and Herod reigned in Jerusalem, there lived in the city of Ecbatana, among the mountains of Persia, a certain man named Artaban, the Median. His house stood close to the outermost of the seven walls which encircled the royal treasury. From his roof he could look over the rising battlements of black and white and crimson and blue and red and silver and gold, to the hill where the summer palace of the Parthian emperors glittered like a jewel in a sevenfold crown.

Around the dwelling of Artaban spread a fair garden, a tangle of flowers and fruit trees, watered by a score of streams descending from the slopes of Mount Orontes, and made musical by innumerable birds. But all color was lost in the soft and odorous darkness of the late September night, and all sounds were hushed in the deep charm of its silence, save the plashing of water, like a voice half sobbing and half laughing under the shadows. High above the trees a dim glow of light shone through the curtained arches of the upper chamber, where the master of the house was holding council with his friends.

He stood by the doorway to greet his guests—a tall, dark man of about forty years, with brilliant eyes set near together under his broad brow, and firm lines graven around his fine, thin lips; the brow of a dreamer and the mouth of a soldier, a man of sensitive feeling but inflexible will—one of those who, in whatever age they may live, are born for inward conflict and a life of quest.

His robe was of pure white wool, thrown over a tunic of silk; and a white, pointed cap, with long lapels at the sides, rested on his flowing black hair. It was the dress of the ancient priesthood of the Magi, called the fire-worshipers.

"Welcome!" he said, in his low, pleasant voice, as one after another entered the room—"welcome, Abdus; peace be with you, Rhadaspes and Tigranes, and with you; my father, Abgarus. You are all welcome, and this house grows bright with the joy of your presence."

There were nine of the men, differing widely in age, but alike in the richness of their dress of many-colored silks and in the massive golden collars around their necks, marking them as Parthian nobles, and in the winged circles of gold resting upon their breasts, the sign of the followers of Zoroaster.

They took their places around a small black altar at the end of the room, where a tiny flame was burning. Artaban, standing beside it, and waving a barsom of thin tamarisk branches above the fire, fed it with dry sticks of pine and fragrant oils. Then he began the ancient chant of the Yasna, and the voices of his companions joined in the beautiful hymn to Ahura-Mazda:

> We worship the Spirit Divine,
>   all wisdom and goodness possessing,
> Surrounded by Holy Immortals,
>   the givers of bounty and blessing,
> We joy in the works of His hands,
>   His truth and His power confessing.
>
> We praise all the things that are pure,
>   for these are His only Creation;
> The thoughts that are true, and the words
>   and deeds that have won approbation;
> These are supported by Him
>   and for these we make adoration.
>
> Hear us, O Mazda! Thou livest
>   in truth and in heavenly gladness;
> Cleanse us from falsehood, and keep us
>   from evil and bondage to badness;
> Pour out the light and the joy of Thy life
>   on our darkness and sadness.

Shine on our gardens and fields,
    Shine on our working and weaving;
Shine on the whole race of man,
    Believing and unbelieving;
    Shine on us now through the night,
    Shine on us now in Thy might,
The flame of our holy love
    and the song of our worship receiving.

The fire rose with the chant, throbbing as if it were made of musical flame, until it cast a bright illumination through the whole apartment, revealing its simplicity and splendor.

The floor was laid with tiles of dark blue veined with white; pilasters of twisted silver stood out against the blue walls; the clear-story of round-arched windows above them was hung with azure silk; the vaulted ceiling was a pavement of sapphires, like the body of heaven in its clearness, sown with silver stars. From the four corners of the roof hung four golden magic-wheels, called the tongues of the gods. At the eastern end, behind the altar, there were two dark-red pillars of porphyry; above them a lintel of the same stone, on which was carved the figure of a winged archer, with his arrow set to the string and his bow drawn.

The doorway between the pillars, which opened upon the terrace of the roof, was covered with a heavy curtain of the color of a ripe pomegranate, embroidered with innumerable golden rays shooting upward from the floor. In effect the room was like a quiet, starry night, all azure and silver, flushed in the east with rosy promise of the dawn. It was, as the house of a man should be, an expression of the character and spirit of the master.

He turned to his friends when the song was ended, and invited them to be seated on the divan at the western end of the room.

"You have come tonight," said he, looking around the circle, "at my call, as the faithful scholars of Zoroaster, to renew your worship and rekindle your faith in the God of Purity, even as this fire has been rekindled on the altar. We worship not the fire, but Him of whom it is the chosen symbol, because it is the purest of all created things. It speaks to us of one who is Light and Truth. Is it not so, my father?"

"It is well said, my son," answered the venerable Abgarus. "The enlightened are never idolaters. They lift the veil of the form and go in to the shrine of the reality, and the new light and truth are coming to them continually through the old symbols."

"Hear me, then, my father and my friends," said Artaban, very quietly, "while I tell you of the new light and truth that have come to me through the most ancient of all signs. We have searched the secrets of nature together, and studied the healing virtues of water and fire and the plants. We have read also the books of prophecy in which the future is dimly foretold in words that are hard to understand. But the highest of all learning is the knowledge of the stars. To trace their courses is to untangle the threads of the mystery of life from the beginning to the end. If we could follow them perfectly, nothing would be hidden from us. But is not our knowledge of them still incomplete? Are there not many stars still beyond our horizon—lights that are known only to the dwellers in the far southland, among the spice-trees and Punt and the gold-mines of Ophir?"

There was a murmur of assent among the listeners.

"The stars," said Tigranes, "are the thoughts of the Eternal. They are numberless. But the thoughts of man can be counted, like the years of his life. The wisdom of the Magi is the greatest of all wisdoms on earth, because it knows its own ignorance. And that is the secret of power. We keep men always looking and waiting for a new sunrise. But we ourselves know that the darkness is equal to the light, and that the conflict between them will never be ended."

"That does not satisfy me," answered Artaban, "for, if the waiting must be endless, if there could be no fulfillment of it, then it would not be wisdom to look and wait. We should become like those new teachers of the Greeks, who say that there is no truth, and that the only wise men are those who spend their lives in discovering and exposing the lies that have been believed in the world. But the new sunrise will certainly dawn in the appointed time. Do not our own books tell us that this will come to pass, and that men will see the brightness of a great light?"

"That is true," said the voice of Abgarus; "every faithful disciple of Zoroaster knows the prophecy of the Avesta and carries the word in his heart. 'In that day Sosiosh the Victorious shall arise out of the number of the prophets in the east country. Around him shall shine a mighty brightness, and he shall make life everlasting, incorruptible, and immortal, and the dead shall rise again.' "

"This is a dark saying," said Tigranes, "and it may be that we shall never understand it. It is better to consider the things that are near at hand, and to increase the influence of the Magi in their own country, rather than to look for one who may be a stranger, and to whom we must resign our power."

The others seemed to approve these words. There was a silent feeling of agreement manifest among them; their looks responded with that indefinable expression which always follows when a speaker has uttered the thought that has been slumbering in the hearts of his listeners. But Artaban turned to Abgarus with a glow on his face, and said:

"My father, I have kept this prophecy in the secret place of my soul. Religion without a great hope would be like an altar without a living fire. And now the flame has burned more brightly, and by the light of it I have read other words which also have come from the fountain of Truth, and speak yet more clearly of the rising of the Victorious One in his brightness."

He drew from the breast of his tunic two small rolls of fine linen, with writing upon them, and unfolded them carefully upon his knee.

"In the years that are lost in the past, long before our fathers came into the land of Babylon, there were wise men in Chaldea, from whom the first of the Magi learned the secret of the heavens. And of these Balaam, the son Beor, was one of the mightiest. Hear the words of his prophecy: 'There shall come a star out of Jacob, and a scepter shall arise out of Israel.'"

The lips of Tigranes drew downward with contempt, as he said:

"Judah was a captive by the waters of Babylon, and the sons of Jacob were in bondage to our kings. The tribes of Israel are scattered through the mountains like lost sheep, and from the remnant that dwells in Judea under the yoke of Rome neither star nor sceptre shall arise."

"And yet," answered Artaban, "it was the Hebrew Daniel, the mighty searcher of dreams, the counsellor of kings, the wise Belteshazzar, who was most honored and beloved of our great King Cyrus. A prophet of sure things and a reader of the thoughts of God, Daniel proved himself to our people. And these are the words that he wrote." (Artaban read from the second roll:) " 'Know, therefore, and understand that from the going forth of the commandment to restore Jerusalem, unto the Anointed One, the Prince, the time shall be seven and three-score and two weeks.' "

"But, my son," said Abgarus, doubtfully, "these are mystical numbers. Who can interpret them, or who can find the key that shall unlock their meaning?"

Artaban answered, "It has been shown to me and to my three companions among the Magi—Caspar, Melchior, and Balthazar. We have searched the ancient tables of Chaldea and computed the time. It falls in this year. We have studied the sky, and in the spring of the year we saw two of the greatest stars draw near together in the sign of the Fish, which is the house of the Hebrews. We also saw a new star there, which shone for one night and then vanished. Now again the two great planets are meeting. This night is their conjunction. My three brothers are watching at the ancient Temple of the Seven Spheres, at Borsippa, in Babylonia, and I am watching here. If the star shines again, they will wait ten days for me at the temple, and then we will set out together for Jerusalem, to see and worship the promised one who shall be born King of Israel. I believe the sign will come. I have made ready for the journey. I have sold my house and my possessions, and brought these three jewels—a sapphire, a ruby, and a pearl—to carry them as tribute to the King. And I ask you to go with me on the pilgrimage, that we may have joy together in finding the Prince who is worthy to be served."

While he was speaking he thrust his hand into the inmost fold of his girdle and drew out three great gems—one blue as a fragment of the night sky, one redder than a ray of sunrise, and one as pure as the peak of a snow mountain at twilight—and laid them out on the outspread linen scrolls before him.

But his friends looked on with strange and alien eyes. A veil of doubt and mistrust came over their faces, like a fog creeping up from the marshes to hide the hills. They glanced at each other with looks of wonder and pity, as those who have listened to incredible sayings, the story of a wild vision, or the proposal of an impossible enterprise.

At last Tigranes said: "Artaban, this is a vain dream. It comes from too much looking upon the stars and the cherishing of lofty thoughts. It would be wiser to spend the time in gathering money for the new fire-temple at Chala. No king will ever rise from the broken race of Israel, and no end will ever come to the eternal strife of light and darkness. He who looks for it is a chaser of shadows. Farewell."

And another said: "Artaban, I have no knowledge of these things, and my office as guardian of the royal treasure binds me here. The quest is not for me. But if thou must follow it, fare thee well."

And another said: "In my house there sleeps a new bride, and I cannot leave her nor take her with me on this strange journey. This quest is not for me. But may thy steps be prospered wherever thou goest. So, farewell."

And another said: "I am ill and unfit for hardship, but there is a man among my servants whom I will send with thee when thou goest, to bring me word how thou farest."

But Abgarus, the oldest and the one who loved Artaban the best, lingered after the others had gone, and said, gravely: "My son, it may be that the light of truth is in this sign that has appeared in the skies, and then it will surely lead to the Prince and the mighty brightness. Or it may be that it is only a shadow of the light, as Tigranes has said, and then he who follows it will have only a long pilgrimage and an empty search. But it is better to follow even the shadow of the best than to remain content with the worst. And those who would see wonderful things must often be ready to travel alone. I am too old for this journey, but my heart shall be a companion of the pilgrimage day and night, and I shall know the end of thy quest. Go in peace."

So one by one they went out of the azure chamber with its silver stars, and Artaban was left in solitude.

He gathered up the jewels and replaced them in his girdle. For a long time he stood and watched the flame that flickered and sank upon the altar. Then he crossed the hall, lifted the heavy curtain, and passed out between the dull red pillars of porphyry to the terrace on the roof.

The shiver that thrills through the earth ere she rouses from her night sleep had already begun, and the cool wind that heralds the daybreak was drawing downward from the lofty, snow-traced ravines of Mount Orontes. Birds, half-awakened, crept and chirped among the rustling leaves, and the smell of ripened grapes came in brief wafts from the arbors.

Far over the eastern plain a white mist stretched like a lake. But where the distant peak of Zagros serrated the western horizon the sky was clear. Jupiter and Saturn rolled together like drops of lambent flame about to blend in one.

As Artaban watched them, behold, an azure spark was born out of the darkness beneath, rounding itself with purple splendors to a crimson sphere, and spiring upward through rays of saffron and orange into a point of white radiance. Tiny and infinitely remote, yet perfect in every part, it pulsated in the enormous vault as if the three jewels in the

Magian's breast had mingled and been transformed into a living heart of light.

He bowed his head. He covered his brow with his hands.

"It is the sign," he said. "The King is coming, and I will go to meet him."

BY THE WATERS OF BABYLON

All night long Vasda, the swiftest of Artaban's horses, had been waiting, saddled and bridled, in her stall, pawing the ground impatiently, and shaking her bit as if she shared the eagerness of her master's purpose, though she knew not its meaning.

Before the birds had fully roused to their strong, high, joyful chant of morning song, before the white mist had begun to lift lazily from the plain, the other wise man was in the saddle, riding swiftly along the high-road, which skirted the base of Mount Orontes, westward.

How close, how intimate is the comradeship between a man and his favorite horse on a long journey. It is a silent, comprehensive friendship, an intercourse beyond the need of words.

They drink at the same wayside springs, and sleep under the same guardian stars. They are conscious together of the subduing spell of nightfall and the quickening joy of daybreak. The master shares his evening meal with his hungry companion, and feels the soft, moist lips caressing the palm of his hand as they close over the morsel of bread. In the gray dawn he is roused from his bivouac by the gentle stir of a warm, sweet breath over his sleeping face, and looks up into the eyes of his faithful fellow-traveler, ready and waiting for the toil of the day. Surely, unless he is pagan and an unbeliever, by whatever name he calls upon his God, he will thank Him for this voiceless sympathy, this dumb affection, and his morning prayer will embrace a double blessing—God bless us both, and keep our feet from falling and our souls from death!

And then, through the keen morning air, the swift hoofs beat their spirited music along the road, keeping time to the pulsing of two hearts that are moved with the same eager desire—to conquer space, to devour the distance, to attain the goal of the journey.

Artaban must indeed ride wisely and well if he would keep the appointed hour with the other Magi; for the route was a hundred and fifty parasangs, and fifteen was the utmost that he could travel in a day. But he knew Vasda's strength, and pushed forward without anxiety, making the fixed distance every day, though he must travel late into the night, and in the morning long before sunrise.

He passed along the brown slopes of Mount Orontes, furrowed by the rocky courses of a hundred torrents.

He crossed the level plains of the Nisaeans, where the famous herds of horses, feeding in the wide pastures, tossed their heads at Vasda's approach, and galloped away with a thunder of many hoofs, and flocks of wild birds rose suddenly from the swampy meadows, wheeling in great circles with a shining flutter of innumerable wings and shrill cries of surprise.

He traversed the fertile fields of Concabar, where the dust from the threshing-floors filled the air with a golden mist, half hiding the huge temple of Astarte with its four-hundred pillars.

At Baghistan, among the rich gardens watered by fountains from the rock, he looked up at the mountain thrusting its immense rugged brow out over the road, and saw the figure of King Darius trampling upon his fallen foes, and the proud list of his wars and conquests graven high upon the face of the eternal cliff.

Over many a cold and desolate pass, crawling painfully across the windswept shoulders of the hills; down many a black mountain-gorge, where the river roared and raced before him like a savage guide; across many a smiling vale, with terraces of yellow limestone full of vines and fruit trees; through the oak groves of Carine and the dark Gates of Zagros, walled in by precipices; into the ancient city of Chala, where the people of Samaria had been kept in captivity long ago; and out again by the mighty portal, riven through the encircling hills, where he saw the image of the High Priest of the Magi sculptured on the wall of rock, with hand uplifted as if to bless the centuries of pilgrims; past the entrance of the narrow defile, filled from end to end with orchards of peaches and figs, through which the river Gyndes foamed down to meet him; over the broad rice-fields, where the autumnal vapors spread their deathly mists; following along the course of the river, under tremulous shadows of poplar and tamarind, among the lower hills; and out upon the flat plain, where the road ran straight as an arrow through the stubble-fields and parched meadows; past the city of Ctesiphon, where the Parthian emperors reigned and the vast metropolis of Seleucia which Alexander built; across the swirling floods of Tigris and the many channels of Euphrates, flowing yellow through the corn-lands—Artaban pressed onward until he arrived at nightfall of the tenth day, beneath the shattered walls of populous Babylon.

Vasda was almost spent, and he would gladly have turned into the city to find rest and refreshment for himself and for her. But he knew that it was three hours' journey yet to the Temple of the Seven Spheres, and he must reach the place by midnight if he would find his comrades waiting. So he did not halt, but rode steadily across the stubble-fields.

A grove of date-plums made an island of gloom in the pale yellow sea. As she passed into the shadow Vasda slackened her pace, and began to pick her way more carefully.

Near the farther end of the darkness an access of caution seemed to fall upon her. She scented some danger or difficulty; it was not in her heart to fly from it—only to be prepared for it, and to meet it wisely, as a good horse should do. The grove was close and silent as the tomb; not a leaf rustled, not a bird sang.

She felt her steps before her delicately, carrying her head low, and sighing now and then with apprehension. At last she gave a quick breath of anxiety and dismay, and stood stock-still quivering in every muscle, before a dark object in the shadow of the last palm-tree.

Artaban dismounted. The dim star-light revealed the form of a man lying across the road. His humble dress and the outline of his haggard face showed that he was probably one of the poor Hebrew exiles who still dwelt in great numbers in the vicinity. His pallid skin, dry and yellow as parchment, bore the mark of the deadly fever which ravaged the marshlands in autumn. The chill of death was in his lean hand, and as Artaban released it the arm fell back inertly upon the motionless breast.

He turned away with a thought of pity, consigning the body to that strange burial which the Magians deemed most fitting—the funeral of the desert, from which the kites and vultures rise on dark wings, and the beasts of prey slink furtively away, leaving only a heap of white bones in the sand.

But, as he turned, a long, faint, ghostly sigh came from the man's lips. The brown, bony fingers closed convulsively on the hem of the Magian's robe and held him fast.

Artaban's heart leaped to his throat, not with fear, but with a dumb resentment at the importunity of this blind delay.

How could he stay here in the darkness to minister to a dying stranger? What claim had this unknown fragment of human life upon his compassion or his service? If he lingered but for an hour he could hardly reach Borsippa at the appointed time. His companions would think he had given up the journey. They would go without him. He would lose his quest.

But if he went on now, the man would surely die. If he stayed, life might be restored. His spirit throbbed and fluttered with the urgency of the crisis. Should he risk the great reward of his divine faith for the sake of a single deed of human love? Should he turn aside, if only for a moment, from the following of the star, to give a cup of cold water to a poor, perishing Hebrew?

"God of truth and purity," he prayed, "direct me in the holy path, the way of wisdom which Thou only knowest."

Then he turned back to the sick man. Loosening the grasp of his hand, he carried him to a little mound at the foot of the palm-tree.

He unbound the thick folds of the turban and opened the garment above the sunken breast. He brought water from one of the small canals near by, and moistened the sufferer's brow and mouth. He mingled a draught of one of those simple but potent remedies which he carried always in his girdle—for the Magians were physicians as well as astrologers—and poured it slowly between the colorless lips. Hour after hour he labored as only a skillful healer of disease can do; and at last the man's strength returned; he sat up and looked about him.

"Who art thou?" he said in the rude dialect of the country, "and why hast thou sought me here to bring back my life?"

"I am Artaban the Magian, of the city of Ecbatana, and I am going to Jerusalem in search of one who is to be born King of the Jews, a great Prince and Deliverer of all men. I dare not delay any longer upon my journey, for the caravan that has waited for me may depart without me. But see, here is all that I have left of bread and wine, and here is a potion of healing herbs. When thy strength is restored thou canst find the dwellings of the Hebrews among the houses of Babylon."

The Jew raised his trembling hand solemnly to heaven.

"Now may the God of Abraham and Isaac and Jacob bless and prosper the journey of the merciful, and bring him in peace to his desired haven. But stay; I have nothing to give thee in return—only this: that I can tell thee where the Messiah must be sought. For our prophets have said that he should be born not in Jerusalem, but in Bethlehem of Judah. May the Lord bring thee in safety to that place, because thou has had pity upon the sick."

It was already long past midnight. Artaban rode in haste, and Vasda, restored by the brief rest, ran eagerly through the silent plain and swam the channels of the river. She put forth the remnant of her strength, and fled over the ground like a gazelle.

But the first beam of the sun sent her shadow before her as she entered upon the final stadium of the journey, and the eyes of Artaban, anxiously scanning the great mound of Nimrod and the Temple of the Seven Spheres, could discern no trace of his friends.

The many-colored terraces of black and orange and red and yellow and green and blue and white, shattered by the convulsions of nature, and crumbling under the repeated blows of human violence, still glittered like a ruined rainbow in the morning light.

Artaban rode swiftly around the hill. He dismounted and climbed to the highest terrace, looking out toward the west.

The huge desolation of the marshes stretched away to the horizon and the border of the desert. Bitterns stood by the stagnant pools and jackals skulked through the low bushes; but there was no sign of the caravan of the wise men, far or near.

At the edge of the terrace he saw a little cairn of broken bricks, and under them a piece of parchment. He caught it up and read: "We have waited past the midnight, and can delay no longer. We go to find the King. Follow us across the desert."

Artaban sat down upon the ground and covered his head in despair.

"How can I cross the desert," said he, "with no food and with a spent horse? I must return to Babylon, sell my sapphire, and buy a train of camels, and provision for the journey. I may never overtake my friends. Only God the merciful knows whether I shall not lose the sight of the King because I tarried to show mercy."

FOR THE SAKE OF A LITTLE CHILD

There was silence in the Hall of Dreams, where I was listening to the story of the Other Wise Man. And through this silence I saw, but very dimly, his figure passing over the dreary undulations of the desert, high upon the back of his camel, rocking steadily onward like a ship over the waves.

The land of death spread its cruel net around him. The stony wastes bore no fruit but briers and thorns. The dark ledges of rock thrust themselves above the surface here and there, like the bones of perished monsters. Arid and inhospitable mountain ranges rose before him, furrowed with dry channels of ancient torrents, white and ghastly as scars on the face of nature. Shifting hills of treacherous sand were heaped like tombs along the horizon. By day, the fierce heat pressed its intolerable burden on the quivering air; and no living creature moved on dumb, swooning earth, but tiny jerboas scuttling through the parched bushes, or lizards vanishing in the clefts of the rock. By night the jackals prowled and barked in the distance, and the lion made the black ravines echo with his hollow roaring, while a bitter blighting chill followed the fever of the day. Through heat and cold, the Magian moved steadily onward.

Then I saw the gardens and orchards of Damascus, watered by the streams of Abana and Pharpar with their sloping swards inlaid with bloom, and their thickets of myrrh and roses. I saw also the long, snowy ridge of Hermon, and the dark groves of cedars, and the valley of the Jordan, and the blue waters of the Lake of Galilee, and fertile plain of Esdraelon, and the hills of Ephraim, and the highlands of Judah. Through all these I followed the figure of Artaban moving steadily onward, until he arrived at Bethlehem. And it was the third day after the three wise men had come to that place and had found Mary and Joseph, with the young child, Jesus, and had laid their gifts of gold and frankincense and myrrh at his feet.

Then the other wise man drew near, weary, but full of hope, bearing his ruby and pearl to offer to the King. "For now at last," he said, "I shall surely find him, though it be alone, and later than my brethren. This is the place of which the Hebrew exile told me that the prophets had spoken, and here I shall behold the rising of the great light. But I must inquire about the visit of my brethren, and to what house the star directed them, and to whom they presented their tribute."

The streets of the village seemed to be deserted, and Artaban wondered whether the men had all gone up to the hill-pastures to bring down their sheep. From the open door of a low stone cottage he heard the sound of a woman's voice singing softly. He entered and found a young mother hushing her baby to rest. She told him of the strangers from the far East who had appeared in the village three days ago, and how they said that a star had guided them to the place where Joseph of Nazareth was lodging with his wife and her newborn child, and how they had paid reverence to the child and given him many rich gifts.

"But the travelers disappeared again," she continued, "as suddenly as they had come. We were afraid at the strangeness of their visit. We could not understand it. The man of Nazareth took the babe and his mother and fled away that same night secretly, and it was whispered that they were going far away to Egypt. Ever since, there has been a spell upon the village; something evil hangs over it. They say that the Roman soldiers are coming from Jerusalem to force a new tax from us, and the men have driven the flocks and herds far back among the hills, and hidden themselves to escape it."

Artaban listened to her gentle, timid speech, and the child in her arms looked up in his face and smiled, stretching out its rosy hands to grasp at the winged circle of gold on his breast. His heart warmed to the touch. It seemed like a greeting of love and trust to one who had journeyed in loneliness and perplexity, fighting with his own doubts and fears, and following a light that was veiled in clouds.

"Might not this child have been the promised Prince?" he asked within himself, as he touched its soft cheek. "Kings have been born ere now in lowlier houses than this, and the favorite of the stars may rise even from a cottage. But it has not seemed good to the God of Wisdom to reward my search so soon and so easily. The one whom I seek has gone before me and I must follow the King to Egypt."

The young mother laid the babe in its cradle, and rose to minister to the wants of the strange guest that fate had brought into her house. She set food before him, the plain fare of peasants, but willingly offered, and therefore full of refreshment for the soul as well as for the body. Artaban accepted it gratefully; and, as he ate, the child fell into a happy slumber, and murmured sweetly in its dreams, and a great peace filled the quiet room.

But suddenly there came the noise of a wild confusion and uproar in the streets of the village, a shrieking and wailing of women's voices, a clangor of brazen trumpets and a clashing of swords, and a desperate cry: "The soldiers! the soldiers of Herod! They are killing our children."

The young mother's face grew white with terror. She clasped her child to her bosom, and crouched motionless in the darkest corner of the room, covering him with the folds of her robe, lest he should wake and cry.

But Artaban went quickly and stood in the doorway of the house. His broad shoulders filled the portal from side to side, and the peak of his white cap all but touched the lintel.

The soldiers came hurrying down the street with bloody hands and dripping swords. At the sight of the stranger in his imposing dress they hesitated with surprise. The captain of the band approached the threshold to thrust him aside. But Artaban did not stir. His face was as calm as though he were watching the stars, and in his eyes there burned that steady radiance before which even the half-tamed hunting leopard shrinks and the fierce bloodhound pauses in his leap. He held the soldier silently for an instant, and then said in a low voice:

"I am all alone in this place, and I am waiting to give this jewel to the prudent captain who will leave me in peace."

He showed the ruby, glistening in the hollow of his hand like a great drop of blood.

The captain was amazed at the splendor of the gem. The pupils of his eyes expanded with desire, and the hard lines of greed wrinkled around his lips. He stretched out his hand and took the ruby.

"March on!" he cried to his men, "there is no child here. The house is still."

The clamor and the clang of arms passed down the street as the headlong fury of the chase sweeps by the secret covert where the trembling deer is hidden. Artaban re-entered the cottage. He turned his face to the east and prayed:

"God of truth, forgive my sin! I have said the thing that is not, to save the life of a child. And two of my gifts are gone. I have spent for man that which was meant for God. Shall I ever be worthy to see the face of the King?"

But the voice of the woman, weeping for joy in the shadow behind him, said very gently:

"Because thou has saved the life of my little one, may the Lord bless thee and keep thee; the Lord make His face to shine upon thee and be gracious unto thee; the Lord lift up His countenance upon thee and give thee peace."

IN THE HIDDEN WAY OF SORROW

Then again there was a silence in the Hall of Dreams, deeper and more mysterious than the first interval, and I understand that the years of Artaban were flowing very swiftly under the stillness of that clinging fog, and I caught only a glimpse, here and there, of the river of his life shining through the shadows that concealed its course.

I saw him moving among the throngs of men in populous Egypt, seeking everywhere for traces of the household that had come down from Bethlehem, and finding them under the spreading sycamore-trees of Heliopolis, and beneath the walls of the Roman fortress of New Babylon beside the Nile—traces so faint and dim that they vanished before him continually, as footprints on the hard river-stand glisten for a moment with moisture and then disappear.

I saw him again at the foot of the pyramids, which lifted their sharp points into the intense saffron glow of the sunset sky, changeless monuments of the perishable glory and the imperishable hope of man. He looked up into the vast countenance of the crouching Sphinx, and vainly tried to read the meaning of the calm eyes and smiling mouth. Was it, indeed, the mockery of all effort and all aspiration, as Tigranes had said—the cruel jest of a riddle that has no answer, a search that never can succeed? Or was there a touch a pity and encouragement in that inscrutable smile—a promise that even the defeated should attain a victory, and the disappointed should discover a prize, and the ignorant should be made wise, and the blind should see, and the wandering should come into the haven at last?

I saw him again in an obscure house of Alexandria, taking counsel with a Hebrew rabbi. The venerable man, bending over the rolls of parchment on which the prophecies of Israel were written, read aloud the pathetic words which foretold the sufferings of the promised Messiah—and the despised and rejected of men, the man of sorrows and the acquaintance of grief.

"And remember, my son," said he, fixing his deep-set eyes upon the face of Artaban, "the King whom you are seeking is not to be found in a palace, nor among the rich and powerful. If the light of the world and the glory of Israel had been appointed to come with the greatness of earthly splendor, it must have appeared long ago. For no son of Abraham will ever again rival the power which Joseph had in the palaces of Egypt, or the magnificence of Solomon throned between the lions in Jerusalem. But the light for which the world is waiting is a new light, the glory that shall rise out of patient and triumphant suffering. And the kingdom which is to be established forever is a new kingdom, the royalty of perfect and unconquerable love.

"I do not know how this shall come to pass, nor how the turbulent kings and peoples of earth shall be brought to acknowledge the Messiah and pay homage to Him. But this I know. Those who seek Him will do well to look among the poor and the lowly, the sorrowful and the oppressed."

So I saw the Other Wise Man again and again, traveling from place to place, and searching among the people of the dispersion, with whom the little family from Bethlehem might, perhaps, have found a refuge. He passed through countries where famine lay heavy upon the land and the poor were crying for bread. He made his dwelling in plague-stricken cities where the sick were languishing in the bitter companion-ship of helpless misery. He visited the oppressed and the afflicted in the gloom of subterranean prisons, and the crowded wretchedness of slave-markets, and the weary toil of galley-ships. In all this populous and intricate world of anguish, though he found none to worship, he found many to help. He fed the hungry, and clothed the naked, and healed the sick, and comforted the captive; and his years went by more swiftly than the weaver's shuttle that flashes back and forth through the loom while the web grows and the invisible pattern is completed.

It seemed almost as if he had forgotten his quest. But once I saw him for a moment as he stood alone at sunrise, waiting at the gate of a Roman prison. He had taken from a secret resting-place in his bosom the pearl, the last of his jewels. As he looked at it, a mellower lustre, a soft and iridescent light, full of shifting gleams of azure and rose, trembled upon its surface. It seemed to have absorbed some reflection of the colors of the lost sapphire and ruby. So the profound, secret purpose of a noble life draws into itself the memories of past joy and past sorrow. All that has helped it, all that has hindered it, is transfused by a subtle magic into its very essence. It becomes more luminous and precious the longer it is carried close to the warmth of the beating heart.

Then, at last, while I was thinking of this pearl, and of its meaning, I heard the end of the story of the Other Wise Man.

A PEARL OF GREAT PRICE

Three-and-thirty years of the life of Artaban had passed away, and he was still a pilgrim, and a seeker after light. His hair, once darker than the cliffs of Zagros, was now white as the wintry snow that covered them. His eyes, that once flashed like flames of fire, were dull as embers smouldering among the ashes.

Worn and weary and ready to die, but still looking for the King, he had come for the last time to Jerusalem. He had often visited the old city before, and had searched through all its lanes and crowded hovels and black prisons without finding any trace of the family of Nazarenes who had fled from Bethlehem long ago. But now it seemed as if he must make one more effort, and something whispered in this heart that at last, he might succeed.

It was the season of the Passover. The city was thronged with strangers. The children of Israel, scattered in far lands all over the world, had returned to the Temple for the great feast, and there had been a confusion of tongues in the narrow streets for many days.

But on this day there was a singular agitation visible in the multitude. The sky was veiled with a portentous gloom, and currents of excitement seemed to flash through a crowd like the thrill which shakes the forest on the eve of a storm. A secret tide was sweeping them all one way. The clutter of sandals, and the soft, thick sound of thousands of bare feet shuffling over the stones, flowed unceasingly along the street that leads to the Damascus gate.

Artaban joined company with a group of people from his own country, Parthian Jews who had come up to keep the Passover, and inquired of them the cause of the tumult, and where they were going.

"We are going," they answered, "to the place called Golgotha, outside the city walls, where there is to be an execution. Have you not heard what has happened? Two famous robbers are to be crucified, and with them another, called Jesus of Nazareth, a man who had done many wonderful works among the people, so that they love him greatly. But the priests and elders have said that he must die, because he gave himself out to be the Son of God. And Pilate has sent him to the cross because he said that he was the 'King of the Jews.'"

How strangely these familiar words fell upon the tired heart of Artaban! They had led him for a lifetime over land and sea. And now they came to him darkly and mysteriously like a message of despair. The King had arisen, but He had been denied and cast out. He was about to perish. Perhaps He was already dying. Could it be the same who had been born in Bethlehem thirty-three years ago, at whose birth the star had appeared in heaven, and of whose coming the prophets had spoken?

Artaban's heart beat unsteadily with that troubled, doubtful apprehension which is the excitement of old age. But he said within himself: "The ways of God are stranger than the thoughts of men, and it may be that I shall find the King, at last, in the hands of His enemies, and shall come in time to offer my pearl for his ransom before He dies."

So the old man followed the multitude with slow and painful steps toward the Damascus gate of the city. Just beyond the entrance of the guardhouse a troop of Macedonian soldiers came down the street, dragging a young girl with torn dress and dishevelled hair. As the Magian paused to look at her with compassion, she broke suddenly from the hands of her tormentors and threw herself at his feet, clasping him around the knees. She had seen his white cap and the winged circle on his breast.

"Have pity on me," she cried, "and save me, for the sake of the God of purity! I also am a daughter of the true religion which is taught by the Magi. My father was a merchant of Parthia, but he is dead, and I am seized for his debts to be sold as a slave. Save me from worse than death."

Artaban trembled.

It was the old conflict in his soul, which had come to him in the palm-grove of Babylon and in the cottage at Bethlehem—the conflict between the expectation of faith and the impulse of love. Twice the gift which he had consecrated to the worship of religion had been drawn from his hand to the service of humanity. This was the third trial, the ultimate probation, the final and irrevocable choice.

Was it his great opportunity or his last temptation? He could not tell. One thing only was clear in the darkness of his mind—it was inevitable. And does not the inevitable come from God?

One thing only was sure to his divided heart—to rescue this helpless girl would be a true deed of love. And is not love the light of the soul?

He took the pearl from his bosom. Never had it seemed so luminous, so radiant, so full of tender, living lustre. He laid it in the hand of the slave.

"This is thy ransom, daughter! It is the last of my treasure which I kept for the King."

While he spoke the darkness of the sky thickened, and shuddering tremors ran through the earth, heaving convulsively like the breast of one who struggles with mighty grief.

The walls of the houses rocked to and fro. Stones were loosened and crashed into the street. Dust clouds filled the air. The soldiers fled in terror, reeling like drunken men. But Artaban and the girl whom he had ransomed crouched helpless beneath the wall of the Praetorium.

What had he to fear? What had he to live for? He had given away the last remnant of his tribute for the King. He had parted with the last hope of finding Him. The quest was over, and it had failed. But even in that thought, accepted and embraced, there was peace. It was not resignation. It was not submission. It was something more profound and searching. He knew that all was well, because he had done the best that he could, from day to day. He had been true to the light that had been given to him. He had looked for more. And if he had not found it, if a failure was all that came out of his life, doubtless that was the best that was possible. He had not seen the revelation of "life everlasting, incorruptible and immortal." But he knew that even if he could live his earthly life over again, it could not be otherwise than it had been.

One more lingering pulsation of the earthquake quivered through the ground. A heavy tile, shaken from the roof, fell and struck the old man on the temple. He lay breathless and pale, with his gray head resting on the young girl's shoulder, and the blood trickling from the wound. As she bent over him, fearing that he was dead, there came a voice through the twilight, very small and still, like music sounding from a distance, in which the notes are clear but the words are lost. The girl turned to see if some one had spoken from the window above them, but she saw no one.

Then the old man's lips began to move, as if in answer, and she heard him say in the Parthian tongue:

"Not so, my Lord: For when saw I thee hungered and fed thee? Or thirsty, and gave thee drink? When saw I thee a stranger, and took thee in? Or naked, and clothed thee? When saw I thee sick or in prison, and came unto thee? Three-and-thirty years have I looked for thee; but I have never seen thy face, nor ministered to thee, my King."

He ceased, and the sweet voice came again. And again the maid heard it, very faintly and far away. But now it seemed as though she understood the words:

"Verily I say unto thee, Inasmuch as thou has done it unto one of the least of these my brethren, thou has done it unto me."

A calm radiance of wonder and joy lighted the pale face of Artaban like the first ray of dawn on a snowy mountain-peak. One long, last breath of relief exhaled gently from his lips.

His journey was ended. His treasures were accepted. The Other Wise Man had found the King.

Henry Van Dyke, 1896

The Gift of the Magi

One dollar and eighty-seven cents. That was all. And sixty cents of it was in pennies. Pennies saved one and two at a time by bulldozing the grocer and vegetable man and the butcher until one's cheeks burned with the silent imputation of parsimony that such close dealing implied. Three times Della counted it. One dollar and eighty-seven cents. And the next day would be Christmas.

There was clearly nothing to do but flop down on the shabby little couch and howl. So Della did it. Which instigates the moral reflection that life is made up of sobs, sniffles, and smiles, with sniffles predominating.

While the mistress of the home is gradually subsiding from the first stage to the second, take a look at the home. A furnished flat at $8 per week. It did not exactly beggar description, but it certainly had that word on the lookout for the mendicancy squad.

In the vestibule below was a letter-box into which no letter would go, and an electric button from which no mortal finger could coax a ring. Also appertaining thereunto was a card bearing the name "Mr. James Dillingham Young."

The "Dillingham" had been flung to the breeze during a former period of prosperity when its possessor was being paid $30 per week. Now, when the income was shrunk to $20, the letters of "Dillingham" looked blurred, as though they were thinking seriously of contracting to a modest and unassuming D. But whenever Mr. James Dillingham Young came home and reached his flat above he was called "Jim" and greatly hugged by Mrs. James Dillingham Young, already introduced to you as Della. Which is all very good.

Della finished her cry and attended to her cheeks with the powder rag. She stood by the window and looked out dully at the gray cat walking a gray fence in a gray backyard. Tomorrow would be Christmas Day, and she had only $1.87 with which to buy Jim a present. She had been saving every penny she could for months, with this result. Twenty dollars a week doesn't go far. Expenses had been greater than she had calculated. They always are. Only $1.87 to buy a present for Jim. Her Jim. Many a happy hour she had spent planning for something nice for him. Something fine and rare and sterling—something just a little bit near to being worthy of the honor of being owned by Jim.

There was a pier-glass between the windows of the room. Perhaps you have seen a pier-glass in an $8 flat. A very thin and very agile person may, by observing his reflection in a rapid sequence of longitudinal strips, obtain a fairly accurate conception of his looks. Della, being slender, had mastered the art.

Suddenly she whirled from the window and stood before the glass. Her eyes were shining brilliantly, but her face had lost its color within twenty seconds. Rapidly she pulled down her hair and let it fall to its full length.

Now, there were two possessions of the James Dillingham Youngs in which they both took a mighty pride. One was Jim's gold watch that had been his father's and his grandfather's. The other was Della's hair. Had the Queen of Sheba lived in the flat across the airshaft, Della would have let her hair hang out the window some day to dry just to depreciate Her Majesty's jewels and gifts. Had King Solomon been the janitor, with all his treasures piled up in the basement, Jim would have pulled out his watch every time he passed, just to see him pluck at his beard from envy.

So now Della's beautiful hair fell about her rippling and shining like a cascade of brown waters. It reached below her knee and made itself almost a garment for her. And then she did it up again nervously and quickly. Once she faltered for a minute and stood still while a tear or two splashed on the worn red carpet.

On went her old brown jacket; on went her old brown hat. With a whirl of skirts and with the brilliant sparkle still in her eyes, she fluttered out the door and down the stairs to the street.

Where she stopped the sign read: "Mme. Sofronie. Hair Goods of All Kinds." One flight up Della ran, and collected herself, panting. Madame, large, too white, chilly, hardly looked the "Sofronie."

"Will you buy my hair?" asked Della.

"I buy hair," said Madame. "Take ye hat off and let's have a sight at the looks of it."

Down rippled the brown cascade.

"Twenty dollars," said Madame, lifting the mass with a practiced hand.

"Give it to me quick," said Della.

Oh, and the next two hours tripped by on rosy wings. Forget the hashed metaphor. She was ransacking the stores for Jim's present.

She found it at last. It surely had been made for Jim and no one else. There was no other like it in any of the stores, and she had turned all of them inside out. It was a platinum fob chain simple and chaste in design, properly proclaiming its value by substance alone and not by meretricious ornamentation—as all good things should do. It was even worthy of The Watch. As soon as she saw it she knew that it must be Jim's. It was like him. Quietness and value—the description applied to both. Twenty-one dollars they took from her for it, and she hurried home with the 87 cents. With that chain on his watch Jim might be properly anxious about the time in any company. Grand as the watch was, he sometimes looked at it on the sly on account of the old leather strap that he used in place of a chain.

When Della reached home her intoxication gave way a little to prudence and reason. She got out her curling irons and lighted the gas and went to work repairing the ravages made by generosity added to love. Which is always a tremendous task, dear friends—a mammoth task.

Within forty minutes her head was covered with tiny, close-lying curls that made her look wonderfully like a truant schoolboy. She looked at her reflection in the mirror long, carefully, and critically.

"If Jim doesn't kill me," she said to herself, "before he takes a second look at me, he'll say I look like a Coney Island chorus girl. But what could I do—oh! what could I do with a dollar and eighty-seven cents?"

At 7 o'clock the coffee was made and the frying-pan was on the back of the stove hot and ready to cook the chops.

Jim was never late. Della doubled the fob chain in her hand and sat on the corner of the table near the door that he always entered. Then she heard his step on the stair away down on the first flight, and she turned white for just a moment. She had a habit of saying little silent prayers about the simplest everyday things, and now she whispered: "Please God, make him think I am still pretty."

The door opened and Jim stepped in and closed it. He looked thin and very serious. Poor fellow, he was only twenty-two—and to be burdened with a family! He needed a new overcoat and he was without gloves.

Jim stopped inside the door, as immovable as a setter at the scent of quail. His eyes were fixed upon Della, and there was an expression in them that she could not read, and it terrified her. It was not anger, nor surprise, nor disapproval, nor horror, nor any of the sentiments that she had been prepared for. He simply stared at her fixedly with that peculiar expression on his face.

Della wriggled off the table and went for him.

"Jim, darling," she cried, "don't look at me that way. I had my hair cut off and sold it because I couldn't have lived through Christmas without giving you a present. It'll grow out again—you won't mind, will you? I just had to do it. My hair grows awfully fast. Say 'Merry Christmas!' Jim, and let's be happy. You don't know what a nice—what a beautiful, nice gift I've got for you."

"You've cut off your hair?" asked Jim, laboriously, as if he had not arrived at that patent fact yet even after the hardest mental labor.

"Cut it off and sold it," said Della. "Don't you like me just as well, anyhow? I'm me without my hair, ain't I?"

Jim looked about the room curiously.

"You say your hair is gone?" he said, with an air almost of idiocy.

"You needn't look for it," said Della. "It's sold, I tell you—sold and gone, too. It's Christmas Eve, boy. Be good to me, for it went for you. Maybe the hairs of my head were numbered," she went on with a sudden serious sweetness, "but nobody could ever count my love for you. Shall I put the chops on, Jim?"

Out of his trance Jim seemed quickly to wake. He enfolded his Della. For ten seconds let us regard with discreet scrutiny some inconsequential object in the other direction. Eight dollars a week or a million a year—what is the difference? A mathematician or a wit would give you the wrong answer. The magi brought valuable gifts, but that was not among them. This dark assertion will be illuminated later on.

Jim drew a package from his overcoat pocket and threw it upon the table.

"Don't make any mistake, Dell," he said, "about me. I don't think there's anything in the way of a haircut or a shave or a shampoo that could make me like my girl any less. But if you'll unwrap that package you may see why you had me going a while at first."

White fingers and nimble tore at the string and paper. And then an ecstatic scream of joy; and then, alas! a quick feminine change to hysterical tears and wails, necessitating the immediate employment of all the comforting powers of the lord of the flat.

For there lay The Combs—the set of combs, side and back, that Della had worshipped for long in a Broadway window. Beautiful combs, pure tortoise shell, with jewelled rims—just the shade to wear in the beautiful vanished hair. They were expensive combs, she knew, and her heart had simply craved and yearned over them without the least hope of possession. And now, they were hers, but the tresses that should have adorned the coveted adornments were gone.

But she hugged them to her bosom, and at length she was able to look up with dim eyes and a smile and say: "My hair grows so fast, Jim!"

And then Della leaped up like a little singed cat and cried, "Oh, oh!"

Jim had not yet seen his beautiful present. She held it out to him eagerly upon her open palm. The dull precious metal seemed to flash with a reflection of her bright and ardent spirit.

"Isn't it a dandy, Jim? I hunted all over town to find it. You'll have to look at the time a hundred times a day now. Give me your watch. I want to see how it looks on it."

Instead of obeying, Jim tumbled down on the couch and put his hands under the back of his head and smiled.

"Dell," said he, "let's put our Christmas presents away and keep 'em a while. They're too nice to use just at present. I sold the watch to get the money to buy your combs. And now suppose you put the chops on."

The magi, as you know, were wise men—wonderfully wise men—who brought gifts to the Babe in the manger. They invented the art of giving Christmas presents. Being wise, their gifts were no doubt wise ones, possibly bearing the privilege of exchange in case of duplication. And here I have lamely related to you the uneventful chronicle of two foolish children in a flat who most unwisely sacrificed for each other the greatest treasures of their house. But in a last word to the wise of these days let it be said that of all who give gifts these two were the wisest. Of all who give and receive gifts, such as they are wisest. Everywhere they are wisest. They are the magi.

O. Henry (William Sydney Porter), 1908

Incident on Fourth Street

One Christmas Eve, when I was a small boy, I was out with my father doing some last-minute errands on Fourth Street in Cincinnati. The packages I was carrying grew heavier with every step, and I could hardly wait to get home so that Christmas could begin.

For this was the night when we three boys trimmed the tree and hung our stockings in front of the fireplace; then the neighbors gathered around our piano for carols so lovely they made a lump in my throat.

It was while I was thinking these things that a hand touched mine. Beside me on the sidewalk stood a bleary-eyed, unshaven, dirty old man, his other hand clutching a ragged cap in which lay a few pennies.

I recoiled from the grimy fingers, turned my shoulder to him, and the old man crept away.

My father had seen. "You shouldn't treat a man that way, Norman," he said.

"Aw, Dad, he's nothing but a bum."

"A bum?" my father said. "There is no such thing as a bum. He is a child of God. Maybe he hasn't made the most of himself, but he is God's beloved child just the same. Now I want you to go and give him this."

My father pulled out his pocketbook and handed me a dollar. This was a large sum for our family; most of our gifts to each other hadn't cost that much. "Now do exactly as I tell you. Go up to him, hand him this dollar, speak to him respectfully, and tell him you are giving him this dollar in the name of Christ."

"Oh, Dad!" I objected, "I couldn't say that!"

My father insisted, "Go and do as I tell you."

Reluctantly, I ran after the old man, caught up with him and said, "Excuse me, Sir, I give you this dollar in the name of Christ."

The old man looked at me in absolute surprise. Then a curious change came over his whole bearing, a new dignity into his manner. Graciously, with a sort of joy, he said, "And I thank you, young Sir, in the name of Christ."

Suddenly the packages in my arms were lighter, the air was warmer, the very sidewalk was beautiful. No Christmas tree stood there, no carols filled the air, but all at once, on Fourth Street, Christmas had begun.

Norman Vincent Peale, 1965

An American, Bill Lederer, wrote the following story/letter, which reflects the power of Christmas. It was published in the Saturday Evening Post *and later in a* Guideposts *magazine Christmas card. Sal Lazzaroti, for many years art director of* Guideposts, *sent the story to me one Christmas.*

A Sailor's Christmas Gift

Chief of Naval Operations
Washington, D.C.

Dear Admiral:

Last year at Christmas time my wife, our three boys and I were in France, on our way from Paris to Nice in a rented car. For five wretched days everything had gone wrong. On Christmas Eve, when we checked into our hotel in Nice, there was no Christmas spirit in our hearts.

It was raining and cold when we went out to eat. We found a drab little restaurant shoddily decorated for the holiday. Only five tables were occupied. There were two German couples, two French families, and an American sailor. While eating, he was writing a letter.

My wife ordered our meal in French. The waiter brought us the wrong thing. I scolded my wife for being stupid.

Then, at the table with the French family on our left, the father slapped one of his children for some minor infraction, and the boy began to cry.

On our right, the German wife began berating her husband.

All of us were interrupted by an unpleasant blast of cold air. Through the front door came an old flower woman. She wore a dripping, tattered overcoat, and shuffled in on wet, rundown shoes. She went from one table to the other.

"Flowers, *Monsieur?* Only one *franc.*" No one bought any.

Wearily she sat down at a table between the sailor and us. To the waiter she said, "A bowl of soup. I haven't sold a flower all afternoon." To the piano player she said hoarsely, "Can you imagine, Joseph, soup on Christmas Eve?"

He pointed to his empty "tipping plate."

The young sailor finished his meal and got up. Putting on his coat, he walked over to the flower woman's table.

"Happy Christmas," he said, smiling and picking out two corsages. "How much are they?"

"Two *francs, Monsieur.*"

Pressing one of the small corsages flat, he put it into the letter he had written, then handed the woman a 20-*franc* note.

"I don't have change, *Monsieur,*" she said. "I'll get some from the waiter."

"No, Ma'am," said the sailor, leaning over and kissing the ancient cheek. "This is my Christmas present to you."

Then he came to our table, holding the other corsage in front of him. "Sir," he said to me, "may I have permission to present these flowers to your beautiful daughter?"

In one quick motion he gave my wife the corsage, wished us a Merry Christmas and departed. Everyone had stopped eating. Everyone had been watching the sailor.

A few seconds later Christmas exploded throughout the restaurant like a bomb.

The old flower woman jumped up, waving the 20-*franc* note, shouted to the piano player, "Joseph, my Christmas present! And you shall have half so you can have a feast too."

The piano player began to belt out *Good King Wenceslaus*.

My wife waved her corsage in time to the music. She appeared 20 years younger. She began to sing, and our three sons joined her, bellowing with enthusiasm.

"Gut! Gut!" shouted the Germans. They began singing in German.

The waiter embraced the flower woman. Waving their arms, they sang in French.

The Frenchman who had slapped the boy beat rhythm with his fork against a glass. The lad, now on his lap, sang in a youthful soprano.

A few hours earlier 18 persons had been spending a miserable evening. It ended up being the happiest, the very best Christmas Eve they ever had experienced.

This, Admiral, is what I am writing you about. As the top man in the Navy, you should know about the very special gift that the U.S. Navy gave to my family, to me and to the other people in that French restaurant. Because your young sailor had Christmas spirit in his soul, he released the love and joy that had been smothered within us by anger and disappointment. He gave us Christmas.

Thank you, Sir, and Merry Christmas!

Bill Lederer, 1963

One Christmas was so meaningful for me that I take the liberty of including its story here. I like to call it "Faraway Christmas."

Faraway Christmas

Golden stars and angels. Festive lights and carols. Shoppers with gaily wrapped packages. Windows glowing with Yuletide pageantry. "Oh," a friend said to me, "aren't they wonderful, all these warm, familiar symbols? Christmas wouldn't be Christmas without them!"

I had to smile a little. Let me tell you why.

Not too long ago, my wife Ruth and the other members of our family—our three children and their spouses and assorted grandchildren—persuaded me that it would be a great adventure to spend Christmas in a completely different setting, one with a totally new atmosphere. "What if we went to Africa," they said with great excitement, "and lived in tents in one of those game parks surrounded by all those wonderful animals? Wouldn't a faraway Christmas be exciting? Wouldn't it be terrific? Wouldn't family ties be strengthened by such a unique experience?"

I protested feebly that perhaps someone who had passed his eighty-seventh birthday, as I had, might find living in a tent surrounded

133

by wild animals a bit strenuous. But no one seemed to be listening. "You'll love every minute of it," Ruth assured me. And so, on this high note of excitement and enthusiasm, we made our preparations to go to East Africa.

The Samburu Game Park in Kenya was indeed far away. And indeed it was different. Ruth and I shared a tent pitched near a fast-flowing brown river. In tents on either side were our children and grandchildren. There was heat and dust and burning sun. At night the forest resounded with barks, screeches, splashes, and once, just behind our tents, a grunting sound that they told me next day had probably been made by a leopard.

So I did not sleep very well, but these unfamiliar things were not what troubled me. What troubled me was that nothing seemed like Christmas. I tried to shrug off the feeling, but it persisted, a kind of emptiness, a sadness almost, a small voice that whispered, "Christmas means coming home, doesn't it? Why have all of you chosen to turn your backs on home like this?"

I did my best to conceal such thoughts from the others, but I couldn't conceal them from myself. And they kept coming back, often at unexpected moments.

On the afternoon of Christmas Eve, for example, we had come back from a splendid day of viewing the animals. We had seen a beautiful herd of zebras, seventy-six elephants, a cheetah chasing an impala, and a nursing lioness, all magnificent in their natural surroundings. Then it was time for a shower before dinner, which was a bit of an adventure, too. The camp helpers heated water, put it in a bucket, then hoisted the bucket to the top of a pole behind the tent. From there the water ran down a pipe into the rear of the tent where, standing on slats, the bather could soap and rinse himself, after a fashion.

I was drying myself off when suddenly—I don't know what triggered it—I found myself remembering long-ago Christmases spent in Cincinnati during my impressionable boyhood years. The city was full of people of German descent, and the Germans are very sentimental about Christmas. I found myself recalling Fountain Square as it looked on Christmas Eve; I thought it the biggest, brightest, most beautiful place I had ever seen. The Christmas tree was enormous, and the streets were alive with carols, many sung in German: *"Stille Nacht"* and *"O Tannenbaum."* I could see myself walking with my father, my small hand in his big one, the snow crunching under our feet. Up on East Liberty Street, where we lived, my mother always had a tree with real candles on it. The smell of those tallow candles mingled with the scent of fir, an aroma unlike any other. Now, standing in our little tent with the vastness of Africa all around me, I remembered that wonderful smell, and I missed it terribly.

We had been told that there would be a special dinner for us that evening. Even this did not cheer me; I thought it might be an artificial occasion with everyone trying too hard to be merry. When I came out near dinnertime, I saw that, in the eating tent, a straggly brown bush had been set up, decorated with small colored lights and some tinsel and red ribbon. I thought of the great tree in Fountain Square and the even greater one in Rockefeller Center in New York City and the magnificent one on the great lawn of the White House in Washington.

We were called to the edge of the river, where chairs had been set up for all of us so that we could see, on the other side, two herders guarding their cattle, their spear tips gleaming like points of light in the gathering dusk. And at the peaceful, almost timeless sight, I felt something stir within me, for I knew that these herders and their charges had not changed in thousands of years. They belonged to their landscape just as the shepherds on the hills outside Bethlehem belonged to theirs. And, at that moment, one of the grandchildren began to sing, hesitantly, tentatively, "O Little Town of Bethlehem." Gradually others joined in with "Hark! the Herald Angels Sing" and then "Joy to the World." Soon we were all singing and, as we sang, everything seemed to change; the sense of strangeness was gone. I looked around the group—our children, their children, singing songs, sharing feelings that in a very real way went back almost 2,000 years to that simple manger in a simple town, with the herders standing by in a parched and primitive land.

Then someone began to read the immortal story from Luke: "And there were in the same country shepherds abiding in the field, keeping watch over their flock by night. . . ." As the story went on, I thought, *How wonderful and simple it is—so wonderful and simple that only God could have thought of it.*

I found myself remembering a radio talk given many years ago by Sam Shoemaker, a much-loved pastor and a good friend of mine. In it, Sam was speculating on what God the Father might have said to Jesus his Son on the night before Jesus left him to go down to earth. He imagined Father and Son conversing much as a human boy and his father might do before the son leaves home to go out into the world. Only Sam, with his great simplicity, could picture it this way. According to this conception, God might have said, "Son, I hate to see you go. I sure am going to miss you. I love you with all my heart. But I do want you to go down to earth and tell those poor souls down there how to live and point them to the way that will lead them back home."

Sam said he thought the last thing God said to Jesus was, "Give them all my love." Now that's simple—but it's human and it's divine.

So when the carols and the Bible reading ended and we walked back to the eating tent for our dinner, I knew with a complete sense of peace that where Christmas is concerned, surroundings do not matter, because the spirit of Jesus is everywhere, knocking on the door of our hearts, asking to be taken in.

The festive lights and the gifts and the ornaments are fine, but they are only a setting for the real jewel: the birth of a Baby that marked the descent of God himself to mankind. That's where the true meaning of Christmas lies. And it can be found in that simple sentence: "Give them all my love."

Norman Vincent Peale, 1990

V.

*Christmas
Thoughts*

*I*N THE PRECEDING pages, we have read the words of Christmas from the Bible, in hymns and carols, in songs and poems, and in stories. But they are also expressed in words we remember from editorials, sermons, letters, plays, and short quotations. And now, to bring this collection of my own favorite words about Christmas to a close, here are some of these other words to bring you joy at Christmas.

Frank Church, editor of the New York Sun, *in 1897 wrote one of the most enduring editorials to appear in an American newspaper. It was captioned*

Is There a Santa Claus?

September 21, 1897

We take pleasure in answering at once and thus prominently the communication below, expressing at the same time our great gratification that its faithful author is numbered among the friends of The Sun:

Dear Editor:

I am 8 years old. Some of my little friends say there is no Santa Claus. Papa says 'If you see it in The Sun it's so.' Please tell me the truth, is there a Santa Claus?

Virginia O'Hanlon
115 West 95th Street

Virginia, your little friends are wrong. They have been affected by the skepticism of a skeptical age. They do not believe except they see. They think that nothing can be which is not comprehensible by their little minds. All minds, Virginia, whether they be men's or children's, are little. In this great universe of ours man is a mere insect, an ant, in his intellect, as compared with the boundless world about him, as measured by the intelligence capable of grasping the whole of truth and knowledge.

Yes, Virginia, there is a Santa Claus. He exists as certainly as love and generosity and devotion exist, and you know that they abound and give to your life its highest beauty and joy. Alas! how dreary would be the world if there were no Santa Claus! It would be as dreary as if there were no Virginias. There would be no childlike faith then, no poetry, no romance to make tolerable this existence. We should have no enjoyment, except in sense and sight. The eternal light with which childhood fills the world would be extinguished.

Not believe in Santa Claus! You might as well not believe in fairies! You might get your papa to hire men to watch in all the chimneys on Christmas Eve to catch Santa Claus; but even if they did not see Santa Claus coming down, what would that prove? Nobody sees Santa Claus, but that is no sign that there is no Santa Claus. The most real things in the world are those that neither children nor men can see. Did you ever see fairies dancing on the lawn? Of course not, but that's no proof that they are not there. Nobody can conceive or imagine all the wonders there are unseen and unseeable in the world.

You tear apart the baby's rattle and see what makes the noise inside, but there is a veil covering the unseen world which not the strongest men that ever lived could tear apart. Only faith, fancy, poetry, love, romance, can push aside that curtain and view and picture the supernal beauty and glory beyond. Is it all real? Ah, Virginia, in all this world there is nothing else real and abiding.

No Santa Claus! Thank God he lives, and he lives forever. A thousand years from now, Virginia, nay, ten times ten thousand years from now, he will continue to make glad the heart of childhood.

Francis Pharcellus Church, 1897

From "A Christmas Sermon"

To be honest, to be kind—to earn a little and to spend a little less, to make upon the whole a family happier for his presence, to renounce when that shall be necessary and not be embittered, to keep a few friends but these without capitulation—above all, on the same grim condition, to keep friends with himself—here is a task for all that a man has of fortitude and delicacy. He has an ambitious soul who would ask more: he has a hopeful spirit who should look in such an enterprise to be successful.

Robert Louis Stevenson, 1888

Cradle Hymn

Away in a manger, no crib for a bed,
The little Lord Jesus laid down His sweet head.
The stars in the bright sky looked down where He lay—
The little Lord Jesus, asleep on the hay.

Martin Luther, 1535

From Hamlet

Some say that ever 'gainst that season comes
Wherein our Saviour's birth is celebrated,
The bird of dawning singeth all night long:
And then, they say, no spirit can walk abroad;
The nights are wholesome; then no plants strike,
No fairy takes, nor witch hath power to charm,
So hallow'd and so gracious is the time.

William Shakespeare, 1602

From "A Christmas Tree"

And I *do* come home at Christmas. We all do, or we all should. We all come home, or ought to come home, for a short holiday—the longer, the better—from the great boardingschool, where we are forever working at our arithmetical slates, to take, and give a rest.

Charles Dickens, 1846

From "Vagabond"

Forget, forgive, for who may say that Christmas day may ever come to host or guest again.

William H. H. Murray, 1872

From "A Thought"

I love the Christmas-tide, and yet,
 I notice this each year I live;
I always like the gifts I get,
 But how I love the gifts I give!

Booth Tarkington, 1921

Long Walk

One of my favorite stories is about a missionary teaching in Africa. Before Christmas, he had been telling his native students how

Christians, as an expression of their joy, gave one another presents on Christ's birthday.

On Christmas morning, one of the natives brought the missionary a seashell of lustrous beauty. When asked where he had discovered such an extraordinary shell, the native said he had walked many miles to a certain bay, the only spot where such shells could be found.

"I think it was wonderful of you to travel so far to get this lovely gift for me," the teacher exclaimed.

His eyes brightening, the native answered, "Long walk, part of gift."

Gerald Horton Bath, 1960

Preface for Christmas Day

Because thou didst give Jesus Christ, thine only Son, to be born at this time for us; who, by the operation of the Holy Ghost, was made very man, of the substance of the Virgin Mary his mother; and that without spot of sin, to make us clean from all sin. Therefore with Angels and Archangels, and with all the company of heaven, we laud and glorify thy glorious Name; evermore praising thee, and saying, Holy,

holy, holy, Lord God of hosts, Heaven and earth are full of thy glory; Glory be to thee, O Lord Most High. Amen.

Book of Common Prayer, 1549

One of the most beloved Roman Catholic popes of our time was Pope John XXIII (1958–63). It is said that when he was elected pope he went back to see his family in the small village where he was born. The people were speechless when they saw him. However, in his kind way, he said, "Don't be afraid. It's only me." In the book Prayers and Devotions from Pope John XXIII, *he wrote about Christmas:*

Christmas Is for the Whole World

How eagerly and lovingly we read the pages of the Sacred Book which describe the birth of Jesus!

A stable, out in the open country, in the darkness of night. Perhaps the gleam of a small lantern. Here is St. Joseph, the just man, chosen by God, here is the Mother of the new-born child, radiant with joy at this surpassing miracle, and here is the divine Babe in the arms of the purest of creatures. He has been so long awaited, through untold ages. But he has come in the hour appointed by God himself. He is tiny, and already subject to the harshest privations, and to suffering: but he is the Word of the Father, the Saviour of the World. The greater the poverty and simplicity, the greater the fascination and appeal of this Child.

Around him the world is stirring: the just have become aware that the great promise is about to be fulfilled. So the day of our redemption dawns, the day of reparation for what is past, of happiness for the eternal future. . . .

The shepherds draw near: they see and feel that peace, joy and love flow out from that tiny Child. The history of twenty centuries begins in this stable, for the Child is in very truth the source of all things. Through him, in fact, everything is renewed, death is overcome, sin is forgiven and Paradise restored.

We feel new fervour of love when we pause in prayer before the Crib.

Mankind also is a great, an immense family. . . . This is proved by what we feel in our hearts at Christmas. The divine Child smiles at everyone; his beloved eyes shine in grace and splendour. Hard hearts are softened, anxieties soothed, suffering relieved.

Calm follows the storm, and sadness ends in joy.

Pope John XXIII, 1966

Acknowledgments

The editor and publisher gratefully acknowledge permission to use copyrighted material in this volume. While every effort has been made to secure permissions, if we have failed to acknowledge copyrighted material, we apologize and will make suitable acknowledgment in any future edition.

American Bible Society for "The Birth of Jesus" from the *Contemporary English Version,* copyright © American Bible Society 1991 and used by permission.

The K. S. Giniger Company, Inc., for "Christmas Is for the Whole World" by Pope John XXIII, from *Prayers and Devotions from Pope John XXIII,* copyright © 1967, 1966 by The K. S. Giniger Company, Inc.

Guideposts Associates, Inc., Carmel, NY 10512, for "The Glory of Christmas" by Laverne Riley O'Brien and "A Christmas List" by Marilyn Morgan Helleberg, reprinted from *The Treasures of Christmas: The Guideposts Family Christmas Book,* copyright © 1982 by Guideposts Associates, Inc.; "A Long Walk" by Gerald Horton Bath and "The